Every one for Truro, Sept. 14, 1897, information about the jubilee and natal celebration

Truro Jubilee and Natal Celebration

The copy filmed here has been reproduced thanks to the generosity of

Nova Scotia Public Archives

L'exemplaire filmé fut reproduit grâce à la générosité de

Nova Scotia Public Archives

The images appearing here are the best quality possible considering the condition and legibility of the original copy and in keeping with the filming contract specifications

Original copies in printed paper covers are filmed beginning with the front cover and ending on the last page with a printed or illustrated impression or the back cover when appropriate All other original copies are filmed beginning on the first page with a printed or illustrated impression, and ending on the last page with a printed or illustrated impression

The last recorded frame on each microfiche shall contain the symbol → (meaning 'CONTINUED''), or the symbol ▽ (meaning END''), whichever applies

Maps, plates, charts, etc , may be filmed at different reduction ratios Those too large to be entirely included in one exposure are filmed beginning in the upper left hand corner, left to right and top to bottom, as many frames as required The following diagrams illustrate the method

Les images suivantes ont été reproduites avec le plus grand soin, compte tenu de la condition et de la netteté de l'exemplaire filmé, et en conformité avec les conditions du contrat de filmage

Les exemplaires originaux dont la couverture en papier est imprimée sont filmés en commençant par le premier plat et en terminant soit par la dernière page qui comporte une empreinte d'impression ou d'illustration, soit par le second plat, selon le cas Tous les autres exemplaires originaux sont filmés en commençant par la première page qui comporte une empreinte d'impression ou d'illustration et en terminant par la dernière page qui comporte une telle empreinte

Un des symboles suivants apparaîtra sur la dernière image de chaque microfiche, selon le cas le symbole → signifie "A SUIVRE", le symbole ▽ signifie FIN''

Les cartes planches, tableaux, etc , peuvent être filmés à des taux de réduction différents Lorsque le document est trop grand pour être reproduit en un seul cliché, il est filmé à partir de l angle supérieur gauche, de gauche à droite, et de haut en bas, en prenant le nombre d'images nécessaire Les diagrammes suivants illustrent la méthode

1	2	3

1
2
3

1	2	3
4	5	6

Every One for Truro

Sept. 14, 1897.

....Information about the....

Jubilee and Natal Celebration.

60th Anniversary of the Reign of QUEEN VICTORIA.		137th Anniversary of the Settlement of TRURO, N. S.

PRINTED AND ISSUED BY THE NEWS PUBLISHING CO., TRURO

TRURO.

It goes without saying, and is acknowledged throughout the Provinces that Truro, situated at the head of the Bay of Fundy, is the first commercial town in Nova Scotia outside of Halifax. Truro is also the railway and educational centre of the Province, offering the best advantages for distributing and wholesale trade and manufacturing, and containing the Provincial Normal, the training school for all the teachers of the public schools Surrounding the town and extending far into the outlying districts is a rich agricultural country. Situated thus, Truro is a solid progressive and steadily growing town, its annual business averaging $8,000,000 a year, and as a home offers a delightfully healthful climate with exceedingly low rates of living. The beauties of Truro are far famed and are a household word in all parts of the Dominion. The streets are lined with beautiful spreading shade trees and all the principal thoroughfares have asphalt side walks. The public buildings, business houses, and private residences fully rival those of all other Maritime towns A most efficient water supply has just been established by which some sixty pounds more pressure, than ever before, has been obtained. The new reservoir has been built at a cost of $15,000 and will furnish a never failing water supply. It is about one and one-half miles from town on the Lepper Brook, about one mile above the Joe Howe falls, A carriage drive has been constructed to the works and it can be visited at any time.

Among the other late improvements and additions is a Home for the Poor and Farm, at a cost of $7,000. These are within one-half mile of town, near what is known as McClure's mills.

The T. A. A. C. grounds and Victoria Park, both important points of interest, especially for Sept. 14th, are referred to elsewhere.

The Chambers' Electric Light and Power Company "turn darkness into light," arc lights being placed at all important points at street corners, etc.

A few of the Industries and advantages, etc., of Truro may be enumerated as follows :

12 churches (with twelve ministers).
Provincial Normal School.
Agricultural College.
$3,000,000 taxable property; 34 miles streets.
Model School; Kindergarten.
Academy and three other schools.
28 Public School Teachers,
Business School; Conservatory of Music.
Y. M. C. A.; W. C. T. U.
Daily newspaper; 4 weekly newspapers.
1 monthly periodical; 3 Job Printing offices.
3 Banking Houses; 14 Hotels.
23 Manufactories; 20 Wholesale firms.
26 Grocery stores; 9 Hardware stores.
9 Dry Goods stores; 2 Furniture stores.
6 Jewellers and Watch repairers' stores.
4 Meat Shops; 6 Shoe stores.
4 Ice Cream and Candy Parlors.
7 Tailor shops; 4 Drug stores.
4 Crockeryware stores.
4 Stationery and Book Stores.
3 Harness and Leather Goods.

...othing and Gents' Furnishing

...eady Made shop.
...ores ; 2 Billiard Rooms
...'s and Decorators' Shops.
... shops ; 4 Photo Studios.
5 ...... Stables ; 1 Plumbing shop.
3 ...le Liveries.
1 ...nhouse.
4 ...aurants.
10 ...iors.
3 D...sts.
14 ...yers.
2 Architects.
1 Steam Laundry.
2 Chinese Laundries
1 Lending Library.
1 Curling Rink.
T A.A.C. Grounds and Club House.
Victoria Park ; Victoria Square.
Brotherhood of St. Andrews.
Mechanics' Institute.
Canadian Order of Forresters.
Two Independent Orders of Forresters.

advantages, etc., of

A Masonic Lodge.
Independent Order of Oddfellows.
Home Circle.
Two Independent Order of Good T
Sons of Temperance.
Diamond Jubilee Temperance Associat ...streets.
Royal Arcanum.
Independent Order of Workmen.
Order of Railway Conductors.
Brotherhood of Trainmen.
Brotherhood of Locomotive Engineers.
Order Railway Telegraphers   ice
Brotherhood Locomotive Firemen.
Order of Railway Trackmen.
Iron Foundry and Machine Shops.
Hat Factory.
Electric Light and Power Station.
Wire Works.

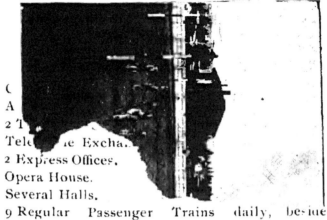

C
A
2 T
Tele...ne Excha...
2 Express Offices.
Opera House.
Several Halls.
9 Regular Passenger Trains daily, besides
    Freights and Specials.
Rifle Range.
Three Fire Engine Houses·
Electric Fire Alarm.
Tennis and Cricket Clubs (ladies and gentlemens)
Bicycle, Baseball. Lacrosse, Football, Hockey
    and Curling Clubs.

A Masonic Lodge.
Independent Order of Oddfellows.
Home Circle.
Two Independent Order of Good T
Sons of Temperance.
Diamond Jubilee Temperance Associa
Royal Arcanum.
Independent Order of Workmen.
Order of Railway Conductors.
Brotherhood of Trainmen.
Brotherhood of Locomotive
Order Railway Telegraphe
Brotherhood Locomotive
Order of Railway T.....

advantages, etc., of

.... streets.

.... in Nova S.....

uro have always been
and are acknowledged
y of the Athletic grounds

Association. Among the Truro boys are found athletes and sportsmen of no mean ability, who, competing, together with the Halifax, Windsor, St. John and Upper Province men, will make an exhibition of the most interesting and exciting nature. The bicycle races will be conducted under the direction of C. W. A. officials, together with men from the T. A. A. C. and the Citizen's General Committee in charge of the whole day's celebration, and universal satisfaction may be expected.

FROM PHOTO BY RICE.

Corner of T. A. A. C. Grounds including Club House and part of Track.

The programme, which will consume the whole afternoon, has been outlined as follows :--

RUNNING RACES.

100 yards dash—1st prize, value $10 ;			2nd, $5.
220 "	"	"	10	"	5.
½ mile run,	"	"	10	"	5.
½ "	"	"	10	"	5.
1 "	"	"	10	"	5.

BICYCLE RACES.

½ mile flying start—1st prize, value $10 ;			2nd, $5.
½ " standing "	"	"	10	"	5.
1 mile novice,	"	"	10	"	5.
1 mile C.W.A. championship of N.S.		15	"	7.
2 mile " "		15	"	7.
2 mile lap race,		12	"	5.

FIELD EVENTS.

Pole vault,	1st prize, value $7 ;		2nd, $3.
Broad jump,	"	"	4	"	2.
High jump,	"	"	4	"	2.
Putting shot,	"	"	4	"	2.
Throwing hammer,	"	"	4	"	2.

In addition to the above, provision has been made to use $35 00 for specially attractive events that had not been decided on when this form was sent to press.

icle

5.
5.
5.
5.
5.

$5.
5.
5.
7.
7.
5.

$3.
2.
2.
2.
2.

)een
ents
was

——

will
ut I

not
keep
:ned
;hly
king
ell's
e no
tion
hon-
man

FROM PHOTO BY RICE.

Truro Amateur Athletic Club House erected 1897 on Club
Grounds at a cost of $2500.00.

FASHIONABLE TAILORING

...BY...

JOHN BRAZIL.

MY SUITS Please the wearer, they
fit perfectly, are made of Superior
Cloths.

PRICES ARE AT ROCK BOTTOM.

When about to get a NEW SUIT call
on me at.........

**CROWN BUILDING,
PRINCE STREET,
TRURO, N. S.**

The handsome T. A. A. C. grounds are enclosed by a high fence and, within, accommodation will be arranged for every visitor in town to witness the above programme. The track on which the races will take place is a quarter of a mile oval cinder track, with a 100 yards straight a way finish opposite the grand stand, and is peer to any track in the Maritime Provinces, numerous Maritime and Provincial records having been taken on it. The new club house is also second to none in Nova Scotia or New Brunswick, and will furnish the best of accommodation to those competing in the sports.

Two bands will furnish music continually during the afternoon, and between events promenading and refreshments may be indulged in.

Any information wanted about this part of the great celebration, not given in this brief outline, or by the general committee, can be obtained from the President of the Club, Mr. C. E. Bentley, or the Secretary and his assistant, Messrs. F. B. Schurman and F. L. Murray.

Victoria Square.

The handsome plot shown by the accompanying cut, is situated between Commercial and Elm and the head of Queen and Prince Streets. Victoria Square is the pride of the citizens and one of the most alluring parts of Truro. It has always been preserved by the town and as far back as the 1770's, when some of the rebellious inhabitants erected a liberty pole and attempted to hold an insurrection meeting here, it was known as the "Parade," and latterly in the seventeenth century and up to 1887 as the "Common." It received its present name, with a grand demonstration in 1887.

Rustic seats are now found everywhere, and surrounding and interlacing the square, under the spreading shade trees, are cool walks largely patronized in summer evenings by promenaders to the Truro Citizens' Band music. A fountain erected by Mr. William Cummings some fifteen years ago sends forth its crystal spray continuously.

Directly opposite and in the near vicinity of this perfect resting place are to be found many of the business houses whose announcements appear in this pamphlet.

ny-
lm
ice of
e of
ays
the
nts
an
the
ary
its
887.

and
the
at
the
ted
ago

of
of
ear

Citizens' Committee for Jub

Executive Officers:—E. E. McNutt, Pres
Mills, Secretary ; G. A. Hall and A. C. M.
McClure, M P.; Hon. F. A. Laurence, Ma

Finance:—E. E. McNutt, A. M. Rennie, H. ?s
S. M. Bentley, R F. Black, Dr. D. H. M

Programme:—A. C. Mills, R. J. Turrer,
W. A. Fitch, Dr. J. H. McKay, John R.

Transportation:—W. E. Bligh, A. C. Mills,
L. B. Archibald, J. E. Price.

Sports and Attractions:—G. A. Hall, D. C
field, John W. Spencer, W. E. Heffernan

Decorations and Illuminations:—W. E.
Crowe, A. S. Black, George H. Leaman, L.
Councillor Rennie, L. R. Rettie, Fran;
McEachran.

Advertising and Press:—G. A. Hall, A. C;
Lunn, A. R. Coffin, G. W. Hopper.

Processions:—A. C. McKenzie, Ross Arc
F. McG. Turner, W. C. Cutten, A. E;
G. Clish, jr., James M. Milne, I. N. Hop;
Smith, J. D. Gladwin, H. T. Walker, W.
Muir White, J. C. Saulnier, Homer McN;

Refreshments:—E. E. McNutt, J. Dover, P
L. B. Crowe, W. D. McCallum, C. Phill

ces—
the
the
e a
ries
ties

gers
Use
ma-
you
our

S.

VICTORIA SQUARE,
Where explosion of Fireworks and Rockets will
Natal Torchlight Procession in the

R. J. TURNER,

Victoria Square,   -   Truro, N. S.

—DEALER IN—

HARDWARE.
Paints, Oils, Glass, Portland Cement and Mechanics Tools.

CROCKERY WARE
and Lamp Goods direct from Manufacturers in the United States, England, France, Austria and Germany.

GROCERIES.
Flour, Feed, Fruits and all general groceries.

WHOLESALE & RETAIL.

Make it a point to visit our show rooms, when at Victoria Square.

RIA SQUARE, TRURO, N. S.
and Rockets will take place, during the great Jubilee and
Procession in the evening—September 14th.

lee and Natal Celebration.

ident ; W. E. Bligh, Treasurer ; Alfred C.
McKenzie —*Honorary Members*.—Firman
M.P.P.; T. G. McMullen, M.P.P.

f. Laurence, W. E. Bligh, A. C. McKenzie,
uir, M. M McLearn.

C. E. Bentley, W. H. Buck, R. T. Craig,
Fisher.

C. M. Dawson, M. Dickie, E. H. Gladwin,

unn, J. D. Ross, W. P. McKay, John Stan-
R. A. Douglas.

Bligh, S. G. Chambers, T. S. Pattillo, H. W.
Dr. W. S. Muir, J. E. Price, F B Schurman,
k Linton, J. M. O'Brien, J. Wright, Angus

Mills, Frank A. Doane, W. B. Alley, C. W.

chibald, Dr. J. H. McKay, William Craig,
. McKay, John Suckling, George Lewis,
per, J. E. Bigelow, C. M. Blanchard, Frank
H. Snook, C. E. Roope, Leonard McKenzie,
Nutt.

McG. Archibald, D. C. Slack, Alex. Miller,
ps, Dr S. L. Walker.

Railway Fares for Sept. 14th.

Exceptionally low passage rates to Truro are being arranged for the celebration. The prices that have been received up to date of publication are as follows :—

Tickets to Truro and return from Amherst $1 50; Nappan, $1.50; Maccan, $1 40; Athol, $1 30; Spring Hill Junction, $1.25; Salt Springs, $1 25; River Philip, $1; Oxford Junction, $1, Thompson, $1: Greenville, 75cts; Westchester 75cts; Wentworth, 65cts; Folly, 50cts; Londonderry, 35cts; East Mines, 35cts: Debert, 25cts; Belmont, 25cts.

From Halifax, $1.25; Rockingham, $1.25, Bedford, $1.25; Windsor Junction, $1; Dartmouth,$1.25; Waverley, $1; Wellington, 85cts; Enfield, 75cts, Elmsdale, 75cts; Milford, 60cts; Shubenacadie, 50cts; Stewiacke, 40cts; Alton, 35cts; Brookfield, 22cts; Hilden, 15cts.

From Pictou, $1 25, Sylvester, $1; Westville,$1; Trenton, $1; New Glasgow, $1; Stellarton, $1; Ferrona Junction, 85cts; Hopewell, 75cts, Glengarry, 65cts; West River, 50cts; Riversdale, 35cts; Valley, 15cts.

A special train from Scotsburn to Oxford will connect with trains from Amherst at proportionate rates From points on the Springhill and Parrs-

---

boro, and Dominion Atlantic Railways, return tickets will be issued at one single first class fare Specially low rates are also under consideration on the steamers from Charlottetown to Pictou.

Sporting men, merchants, and others may procure tickets at single first class fare, together with a standard certificate, at *all* stations on I. C. R., Moncton, St. John, Levis, Sydney and elsewhere. Such tickets will entitle holder to return ticket free, if same be endorsed by Secretary of celebration, commencing 13th or 14th, returning 15th September.

On arrival at Truro station cabs can be secured at little cost for any part of town where attractions are going on.

Gunn's Opera House

FROM PHOTO BY RICE.

This modern and finely equipped Opera House, on Inglis Street, was opened June 26th, 1894, and has, thus soon, gained a high rank among such buildings in the Maritime Provinces. The stage is 40x22 feet and 20 feet high, and fitted with exquisite scenery. The main building and gallery are seated with folding chairs, sufficient to accommodate 850 persons. The hall is lighted by electricity and has perfect ventilation.

Somerby's Theatre of twelve Dwarfs will give two performances here on the 14th—afternoon and evening. This show is of a character of vital interest, and is one of the few that should never be missed, when an opportunity is given to see them.

Brief Information of Programme.

The Truro Jubilee and Natal celebration on Sept. 14th, will begin at 7 o'clock, after an early breakfast, by the ringing of bells, blowing of steam whistles, horns, and all sorts of noisy instruments, and the firing of salutes, followed by a general parade of Calithumpians and Polymorphians.

At 1 o'clock the great procession of the day will start from the Railway Esplanade, traversing Walker, Prince, Elm and Queen Streets, with probable digressions onto nearly all the other important thoroughfares and streets of the town. The extent of this parade will be unlimited and will include manufacturers', tradesmen's, newspapermen's, railwaymen's, fraternal societies, and school children's display, and three at least, probably more, bands of music.

If all the other attractions that are offered come up to the anticipation of the committee in charge —and there is every assurance that they will—this procession will last about one hour and, alone, will be a sight of a life time to many.

At two o'clock the immense crowd will divide into at least three sections—one section for the T.A.A.C. grounds to witness the sports; another section for Victoria Park, to take in the Railway Picnic, and still another to Gunn's Opera House to see and hear Somerby's Dwarfs—all of which are referred to and illustrated elsewhere.

When the afternoon has been spent, and lunch or tea partaken of, the crowds will again swarm the streets to witness a grand illuminated and torch light procession, that will start from the Railway Esplanade at 7 o'clock. This procession, although perhaps not so large as the afternoon one, will be most attractive. It will be led by the Century Cycle Club, with illuminated wheels, and will also include the firemen's display, which is being arranged at considerable cost, bands of music and very extensive and unusual fire works. All public and private buildings along the route and throughout town will vie with each other in their illuminations and decorations At Victoria Square, a picture of which is given elsewhere, extra fireworks will be played and rockets exploded. Penny's Mountain, Wimburn Hill, and all elevations surrounding the town, will be lighted by bonfires.

This procession will lead at 8.30 o'clock, to the two principal points of the evening's attractions, viz., Gunn's Opera House, and Victoria Park. At the former a Jubilee Souvenir performance will be given, and at the latter, an illuminated promenade concert will take place and the principal fireworks of the day will be operated.

Simultaneously at 11 p m. the day's amusements will be called off, and the signal be given for visitors that their train time has arrived, by singing the National Anthem.

During the whole day, perhaps with exception of an hour or so for the Trade procession, all places of business will be open and merchants, coming from a distance, will receive prompt attention from their wholesale dealers, as will also the retail trade at the hands of the obliging clerks of the different fully equipped and up to date stores of the town. New Fall Goods will be in, and no better opportunity for people, all over the Province to save money by purchasing winter supplies from the Hub of the Province can be offered.

NOTE·—Procession announced at 1 o'clock, on previous page, should read 10 o'clock a m

Victoria Park.

This picturesque and romantic Park has more than a Provincial reputation. Railway guides, books of travel and newspaper articles by the hundreds have descanted upon the unequalled beauty of Truro's Park. All visitors to the town to take in the Natal Day proceedings, must visit this spot and enjoy the beauties of a natural gorge between lofty hills with rugged sloping sides that have been so much admired by thousands, whose wide extended travel in foreign lands, amid the beauties of Nature's most lavish gifts, make their good opinion of great value in regard to the perfection of this gem of a Park.

FROM PHOTO BY RICE.

Band Pavillion. Victoria Park.

Leading almost directly south from the railway station, a wide level expanse of low ground with rich velvet carpet of green suddenly converge into narrow limits guarded on each side by trees clad hills, that, as the valley contracts its limits, rise up with their everlasting peaks as stern sentinels over the peaceful shades below. Through this lovely valley leaps from rock to rock with al-

most confusing windings a thread-like silvery
stream that can be crossed in numberless places by
artistic and romantic bridges and can be followed
in its serpentine course along shaded walks skil-
fully constructed at the base of the great rocks
that tower threateningly skywards There is a
combination of glen and gorge, of hill and dale, of
the beautiful and the grand, of light and shadow,
that once seen will be a green spot to be ever cher-
ished and brought up in pleasing memory.

FROM PHOTO BY RICE

True Lovers Bridge, Victoria Park

As one pierces the dark sylvan retreat, the low
roaring of falling water bursts on the ear, and at a
sharp turn in the rising footpath suddenly appears
the tumbling cascade, the well known "Joe Howe
Falls" The great Howe has embalmed all this
scene in his poetic prose language, the grandest
enconium this beauty spot has ever received.
Further up the dashing stream are other but
smaller cascades, whose waters wildly chase one
another for their playful leap into the boiling
chaldron beneath the Howe Falls A walk yet
further beyond will bring the visitor to the grand
reservoir, hidden among the hills, that is to supply
Truro's growing population with the water required for domestic and fire purposes.

But no one must leave this romantic Park without wandering among the intricate mazes and many labyrinths constructed by the ingenuity of Mr. Jas. D. Ross, one of Truro's most patriotic citizens, who deserves all the credit for the attractive appearance to day of Truro's Park

Let the visitor in wandering about this Park interest himself in trying to locate the "Lily Caldron," "the Holy Well," "Nymph's Grotto," "The Sphinx," "Three old Bachelors," " Engagement Seat," and the many other things of interest and objects of history that everywhere dot this pretty Park. Hours can be spent here with profit and pleasure.

Railway Men's Picnic.

Not only will citizens celebrate Natal Day and the Diamond Jubilee of Queen Victoria in Truro on September 14th, but a large body of railway men—about 1500—will hold a railway picnic in Victoria Park. They will join in the processions and celebration proceedings afternoon and evening and in the afternoon will carry out the following programme of sports in the Park :—

1. Grand championship tug-of-war between teams of railway men weighing 1600 lbs. Prizes, Gold Jubilee medal for each in winning team

2. Tug of-war between teams of men (all comers) weighing 1800 lbs. Prizes, silver medals.

3. 100 yards dash—amateur, railway men.

4. 100 yards dash—open to all comers.

5. Running broad jump—open to railway men.

6. Three-legged race—open to railway men.

7. Hop skip and jump—open to all comers.

8. Egg and table race—open to railway men.

9. Running high jump—open to railway men.

10. Boys' race open to railway men's boys, 13 years of age and under.

11. Girls' race open to railway men's girls, 13 years of age and under.

12—Little girls' race—open to railway men's children, 10 years old and under

A military band will be in attendance, and refreshments and cooling drinks will be obtainable.

CPSIA information can be obtained at www.ICGtesting.com
Printed in the USA
BVOW07s1657180214

345292BV00009B/202/P

SCHOLASTIC

Multimodal Texts

Digital texts for on-screen literacy lessons

Year 2

Scottish Primary Y3

Author

Karen Mawer

Development Editor

Rachel Mackinnon

Editor

Vicky Butt

Assistant Editor

Alex Albrighton

Series Designers

Micky Pledge and Melissa Leeke

Designer

Micky Pledge

CD-ROM development

CD-ROM developed in association with Infuze Ltd

Acknowledgements

The publishers gratefully acknowledge permission to reproduce the following copyright material:

Forces and *Clean-up day* and *Plant art* websites by Sarah Fleming © 2008, Sarah Fleming (2008, previously unpublished). *The Ring* by Adam Guillain © 2008, Adam Guillain (2008, previously unpublished). *The Rabbit and the Fox* by Fiona Undrill © 2008, Fiona Undrill (2008, previously unpublished). *Toads and Diamonds* by Clare Robertson © 2008, Clare Robertson (2008, previously unpublished). *Skipping and kicking!* by Sue Graves © 2008, Sue Graves (2008, previously unpublished). *Football in the park* by Celia Warren © 2008, Celia Warren (2008, previously unpublished). Extracts from Primary National Strategy's *Primary Framework for Literacy* (2006) www.standards.dfes.gov.uk/primaryframework © Crown copyright. Reproduced under the terms of the Click Use Licence.

Every effort has been made to trace copyright holders for the works reproduced in this book, and the publishers apologise for any inadvertent omissions.

Published by Scholastic Ltd
Villiers House
Clarendon Avenue
Leamington Spa
Warwickshire CV32 5PR
www.scholastic.co.uk

Designed using Adobe InDesign.

Printed in China through Golden Cup Printing Services

1 2 3 4 5 6 7 8 9   8 9 0 1 2 3 4 5 6 7

Text © 2008 Karen Mawer
© 2008 Scholastic Ltd

British Library Cataloguing-in-Publication Data
A catalogue record for this book is available from the British Library.
ISBN 978-1407-10013-5

Minimum system requirement:

- PC or Mac with a 4x speed CD-ROM drive and 512MB RAM
- Windows 98/2000/XP or Mac OSX 10.2 or later
- Recommended minimum processor speed 900Mhz
- 16bit sound and graphics card

Contents

Introduction

What are multimodal and digital texts?

Multimodal texts include at least two of the following:
- written text
- images
- sound
- movement or gesture.

Digital texts are those which are electronic.

A digital text does not have to be multimodal and a multimodal text does not have to be digital.

Why teach them?

Multimodal texts are all around us, from picture books to information leaflets, and children are exposed to a large amount of digital information through the internet, computer games, television and so on. The DfES document *Multimodal – ICT – Digital texts* says *The texts children read on screen influence their writing.* These texts and their features need to be studied alongside traditional texts. The Revised Literacy Framework recommends that multimodal or digital elements are incorporated into literacy teaching through the use of digital cameras, sound recording software, presentational software and so on. *Multimodal Texts* allows you and your children to explore these text types in a safe environment.

About the product

The CD-ROM provides:

- Three mini-websites – completely self-contained with live links including photographs, video or audio.
- Video – a short film with narration.
- Animation – moving illustration with voice-over.
- Three stories – one with an alternative ending (decide as a class what the characters chose to do), all fully illustrated with audio versions.
- Playscript – with full audio version to listen to and with individual sound effects to use in whole-class re-enactment.
- Poetry – fully illustrated with audio version.
- Podcast and audio – both with a transcript which scrolls as you listen and a PDF version to print.
- Two sequences of images – listen to the related sound effects by clicking on the buttons.
- Photocopiable pages (also provided in the book).

The book contains detailed teaching ideas based on the CD-ROM texts.

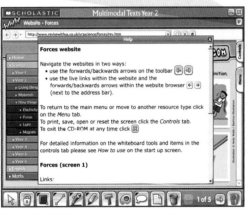

About the CD-ROM

The CD-ROM is installable; follow the text file instructions on the disk to install it on to your system. Once installed, navigate to the program location to open it.

Help
Below are brief guidance notes for using the CD-ROM. For more detailed information see *How to use* on the start-up screen, or see '?' for screen-by-screen help (top right-hand corner of the screen).

Main menu
This screen provides links to all the text types and the photocopiable pages. Click on a text type button to be taken either to the sub-menu or directly to that resource.

Menu

The menu tab on the right-hand side of the screen allows you to navigate to other areas on the CD-ROM. Click on the tab to open the menu.

Main Menu
Websites
Video
Animation
Stories
Playscript
Poetry
Podcast
Audio
Images

Printing

All of the resources are printable. For websites, stories, playscripts, poetry and images there are two print options. You can either print the current screen, including annotations (unless annotations are hidden) or you can print a clean set of the entire resource (every screen). For all other resources the current screen will print with any annotations.

Print current screen

Print all screens in current activity

Cancel

Controls

Click on the controls tab on the right-hand side of the screen to access the Print, Open, Save and Reset-screen buttons.

Whiteboard tools
The CD-ROM comes with its own set of whiteboard tools for use on any whiteboard. These include:

Print (see Printing for more information).

Save all annotations you have made to the texts.

Open – navigate to your saved file to open your annotations.

Reset the page.

Pen tool – draw freehand in three different thicknesses.

Shape tool – add a filled or unfilled circle or square.

Speech/thought bubbles – add a speech or thought bubble.

Text tool – add text using the keyboard.

Rubbish bin – select an annotation and click this button to delete it.

Select tool.

Annotations – on and locked/ hidden and locked/unlocked.

Line tool – draw straight lines in three different thicknesses.

Highlighter tool – highlight in three different thicknesses.

Colour palette – select a colour to annotate in.

Notes – add a sticky-note style box to type in.

Forwards/backwards – navigate between the text pages.

Volume – adjust the volume using the slider, or mute by clicking the speaker icon.

1 of 4

Please note – to access buttons on screen, such as playback buttons, the padlock needs to be in the locked position.

Forces

Objectives

● Strand 3: Listen to each other's views and preferences, agree the next steps to take and identify contributions by each group member.
● Strand 7: Explain organisational features of texts, including alphabetical order, layout, diagrams, captions, hyperlinks and bullet points.

Differentiation

Support
● Give the children the photographs from the experiment to put into the correct order. They can add a caption to each one. Ask them to explain orally what they discovered, as an adult scribes.
Extend
● Challenge the children to write a paragraph to explain how they carried out the experiment, using the photographs as visual prompts. Encourage the use of sequential steps, time and causal connectives, and the past tense.

Cross-curricular activities

Science Unit 2E
Forces and movement
● Investigate how to make beanbags and balls move faster or slower or change direction. Record ideas on paper using diagrams and words.
Design and technology Unit 2A Vehicles
● Make model vehicles with moving axles. Roll them down ramps and see which one travels the furthest.

How the text works and responding to the text

● This website is for children to use as a revision tool when they have completed a unit of work about forces. Before looking at it, revise with the class what they already know about forces.

● As the website is explored, teach the children the technical names for hyperlinks, pop-up boxes and menus, and explain how they work.

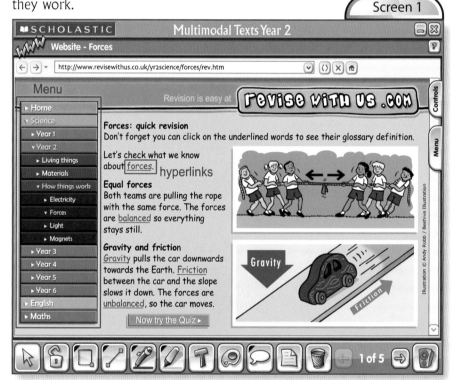

● Look at screen 1 and identify the web address, compare this to the location of a book in a library. Look at the menu, discuss how it would work (please note the menu is not active) and what else could be found on the website. Compare it to a book index and how it is organised.

● Read the information on screen 1. Note how text and images are being used to convey information. Point out the hyperlinks to the glossary and compare this to the way glossary words are shown in a book.

● Before looking at the glossary, challenge pairs to write definitions for each of the words on individual whiteboards. Then click on a glossary word and look at the pop-up. Note that it is in alphabetical order as a book glossary would be. Evaluate the children's glossary definitions against the definitions on the website.

● Ask each pair to work together to complete the quiz on screen 2 of the website. Discuss the answers.

Writing activities

● Carry out an investigation with the children entitled 'Cars rolling down a ramp'. You will need a variety of toy

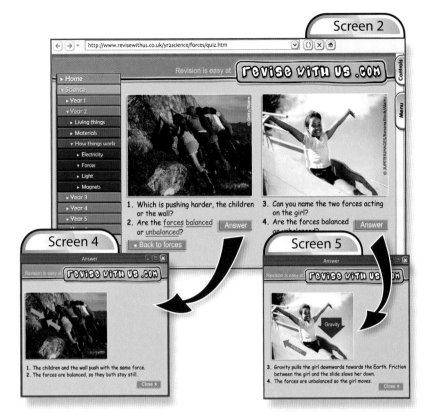

Screen 2

http://www.revisewithus.co.uk/yr2science/forces/quiz.htm

Revision is easy at **revise with us .com**

- Home
- Science
  - Year 1
  - Year 2
    - Living things
    - Materials
    - How things work
      - Electricity
      - Forces
      - Light
      - Magnets
  - Year 3
  - Year 4
  - Year 5

1. Which is pushing harder, the children or the wall?
2. Are the <u>forces</u> <u>balanced</u> or <u>unbalanced</u>? [Answer]
   ◄ Back to forces

3. Can you name the two forces acting on the girl?
4. Are the forces balanced or unbalanced? [Answer]

Screen 4

Answer

Revision is easy at **revise with us .com**

1. The children and the wall push with the same force.
2. The forces are balanced, so they both stay still.
   [Close x]

Screen 5

Answer

Revision is easy at **revise with us .com**

Gravity

3. Gravity pulls the girl downwards towards the Earth. Friction between the girl and the slide slows her down.
4. The forces are unbalanced so the girl moves.
   [Close x]

cars, blocks to build up the ramps, ramps of equal length but with different surfaces, and measuring equipment.

- Split the class into three groups. Challenge one group to find out how the size of the car affects the distance travelled down a ramp. Challenge another group to find out how the height of the ramp affects the distance a car travels. Challenge the final group to find out how the ramp surface affects the distance a car travels.

- Encourage the groups to plan their experiment together as a team. Point out that each team member should have an opportunity to give their suggestions while the rest of the team listens. Insist that the groups reach an agreement about what they are going to do and explain it to you before they can begin the experiment. Ask each group questions to help them consider fair testing.

- Ask each group to carry out their experiment and record their results in a table. Give a format for this. Take photographs of each step of the experiments to use later. (Remember to get parents' or carers' permission before taking photographs of the children.) As they work, ask the groups to identify which children contributed specific ideas.

- Supply each child with a copy of photocopiable page 34 'Cars on a ramp'. Ask them to use it to create a flow chart to show pictorially what they did in their experiment. Add captions to each drawing.

- Support the children in creating individual web pages to explain their experiment and their findings. Give each child an electronic template to complete with the following headings and layout: 'The experiment' (add the photographs taken earlier beneath the heading then leave space for caption text to be added to each one), 'The results' (add an appropriate table with space for results to be added), 'The conclusion' (leave space for a paragraph of text to explain what was found out). Model each section before the children begin to complete it.

- Invite some of the children to display their web pages on the interactive whiteboard then present their findings orally to the class.

Whiteboard tools

- Whiteboard tools used on the screen shots include:
  - ▢ Outline box
  - T Text tool
  - ◉ Colour used ●

Assessment

- Observe which children worked well in their group and were able to offer their ideas, take turns and listen to the ideas of others.
- Can the children explain the organisational features of a website such as the menu, hyperlinks and pop-up boxes?

Reference to _100 Literacy Framework Lessons_

- Non-fiction Unit 2 Explanations pages 107–122

Photocopiable

- See page 34 or CD-ROM.

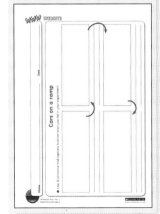

Cars on a ramp

Clean-up day

Objectives

● Strand 7: Draw together ideas and information from across a whole text, using simple signposts in the text.
● Strand 11: Use question marks, and use commas to separate items in a list.

Differentiation

Support
● The children can create their leaflet using a video camera. They could commentate over a video of a local clean-up day and interview the children that took part.
Extend
● Ask the children to plan their leaflet without the help of the photocopiable sheet. Suggest that they create their own mind map, considering the headings they would like on each page of the leaflet and then making notes under each of these headings.

Cross-curricular activities

ICT Unit 2A
Writing stories and Unit 2B Creating pictures
● Ask the children to create a poster to advertise a clean-up day. Encourage them to use words and pictures to display their message. Talk about the important information that is needed on the poster.

Whiteboard tools

● Whiteboard tools used on the screen shots include:
✎ Pen tool
◉ Colour used ●

How the text works and responding to the text

● These three web pages are taken from a website about local environmental issues. They instruct people how to organise a local clean-up day.

● Briefly explain what a clean-up day is and then ask the class to generate some questions that they would like to find out about clean-up days. Give the children a variety of question words to begin their questions with – for example, 'what', 'where', 'how' – and model how to use question marks at the end of a question. Keep the questions so they can be answered later.

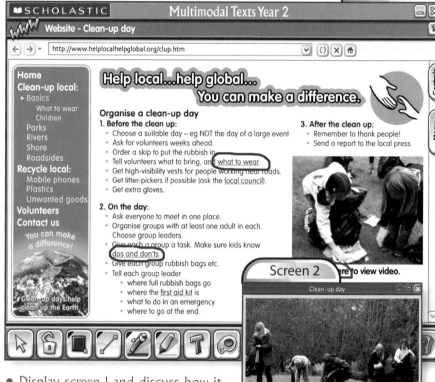

● Display screen 1 and discuss how it can be navigated via menus, buttons and hyperlinks.

● Allow each child time to read the information on all of the screens individually and to talk to a partner about what they have discovered.

● Set the children the task of answering, on their own, the following question using the website: *What clothes should I wear on clean-up day?* Ask them to explain how they found the answer. (By following the hyperlink *what to wear* from the main page.)

● Ask each child to make a list to take home for their parents showing the equipment they will need to have on clean-up day. Model how to use commas to separate items in a list and ask the children to prepare their list in the same way.

● Refer the children back to the questions they created earlier and challenge them to find the answers on the website. Talk about the ease of use of the website for finding information and compare this to finding information in a book.

- Involve the whole class in organising a clean-up day in your local area. Model how to use the website as a source of information.

Writing activities

- Tell the children that they are responsible for making a leaflet about clean-up days so that other schools can organise and hold one too.

- Consider the main information that people would need to know if they were going to have a clean-up day — what it is, how to organise one and how to keep the children safe. Create a set of criteria that the leaflet must meet.

- Give a copy of photocopiable page 35 'Clean-up day' to each pair of children and ask them to make notes from the website (and other sources if available) under each of the three headings. Emphasise, by modelling, that notes are created using key words and phrases. Discourage the children from copying out whole sentences and chunks of text.

- Working individually, tell the children to fold a piece of A4 paper in half to create a leaflet. Share ideas about how the front cover of the leaflet should look and then ask each child to design their own front cover. Tell them to put one of the three headings from the photocopiable at the top of each of the remaining pages.

- Model how to turn notes into coherent present-tense sentences that give information. Support the children in writing a paragraph of information under each heading in their leaflets.

- Consider how pictures and diagrams can also give information. As a class, generate ideas for pictures or diagrams that could be used to enhance the information already given, then encourage each child to add these to their leaflets.

- As a class, evaluate the finished leaflets against the set of criteria created at the beginning of the task. Revise the leaflets if necessary to improve them and then re-evaluate them.

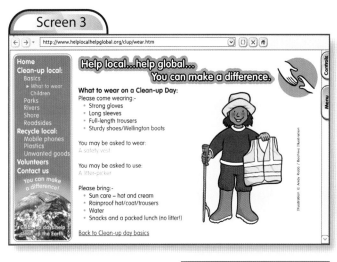

Screen 3

http://www.helplocalhelpglobal.org/club/wear.htm

Home
Clean-up local:
  Basics
  ▶ What to wear
  Children
  Parks
  Rivers
  Shore
  Roadsides
Recycle local:
  Mobile phones
  Plastics
  Unwanted goods
Volunteers
Contact us
You can make a difference!

Help local...help global...
You can make a difference.

What to wear on a Clean-up Day:
Please come wearing:-
- Strong gloves
- Long sleeves
- Full-length trousers
- Sturdy shoes/Wellington boots

You may be asked to wear:
A safety vest

You may be asked to use:
A litter-picker

Please bring:-
- Sun care – hat and cream
- Rainproof hat/coat/trousers
- Water
- Snacks and a packed lunch (no litter!)

Back to Clean-up day basics

Screen 4

http://www.helplocalhelpglobal.org/club/kids.htm

Home
Clean-up local:
  Basics
    What to wear
  ▶ Children
  Parks
  Rivers
  Shore
  Roadsides
Recycle local:
  Mobile phones
  Plastics
  Unwanted goods
Volunteers
Contact us
You can make a difference!

Help local...help global...
You can make a difference.

Dos and don'ts for kids on clean-up day

Dos
Make sure children:
- put litter in a rubbish bag.
- stay with the group.
- tell an adult if they find:
  - broken glass
  - sharp metal (eg an old bike wheel).

Keep a close eye on children near a:
- river
- road

All day remember to make sure children:
- drink water.
- eat when they're hungry.
- put on more sun cream if it's sunny.
- do what their group leader tells them.

Make sure everyone has fun!

Back to Clean-up day basics

Don'ts
Make sure children don't:
- fill their rubbish bag so full they can't carry it.
- go off on their own.
- touch anything dangerous.

Assessment

- Once the children have generated some questions about a clean-up day there is an opportunity to assess their ability to read for meaning and for a purpose as they try to find the answers on the website.
- Assess the children's independent use of question marks by asking them to write one question about the clean-up day before demonstrating how to use them accurately. This will give a baseline of children's understanding of question marks before the lesson.

Reference to
100 Literacy Framework Lessons

- Non-fiction Unit 3 Information texts pages 123–140

Photocopiable

- See page 35 or CD-ROM.

Objectives

● Strand 7: Draw together ideas and information from across a whole text, using simple signposts in the text.
● Strand 11: Compose sentences using tense consistently.

Differentiation

Support
● Invite the children to create a group page for the book. For further support, provide a writing frame.
Extend
● Challenge the children to create a glossary to add to their books. Ask them to highlight five words in their text that might need defining, order them alphabetically, then write a definition for each word.

Cross-curricular activities

Art and design Unit 2B Mother Nature – designer
● Cut some pieces of fruit in half. Ask the children to use colouring pencils to draw the inside of the fruits. Encourage them to create a collage that clearly represents the textures they observed.

Whiteboard tools

● Whiteboard tools used on the screen shots include:
📄 Sticky notes
🖉 Colour used ●

Plant art

How the text works and responding to the text

● These web pages are from an art website aimed at children. They incorporate images of artwork from established artists who have used plants as a stimulus for their work. The bright, fun appearance of the pages has been designed with children as the main audience.

● Show the children screens 1 and 4 of the website and ask them to look closely and decide what the website is about. Encourage them to look at the web address, menu, headings, text and images to make sensible predictions. Allow the children time to discuss their ideas with a partner before sharing them with the class. Ask them to explain the reasons for their ideas by referring back to the website.

● Look at the functionality of the website – the buttons, menus and hyperlinks. Revise the technical names and the function of these items. Compare this to a book about artwork. Look at the advantages and disadvantages of each for a range of purposes.

● Discuss individual reactions to the pieces of artwork shown. Ask: *What does the artwork show? What materials do you think were used? How was the artwork created? Who created it? Do you like the artwork? Why?*

● The answers to the website questions are as follows: the lino print picture is stylised, showing veins/cells and so on; its realism is limited by the restrictions of the medium. Children can identify the strawberry plants in the unicorn painting by comparing the one in the close-up with the botanical drawing. They can then look for other strawberry plants in the tapestry — there are quite a few.

● Look at the way the website author has written about the pieces of artwork. Note that they have written factual sentences in the present tense. Construct some non-fiction sentences with the class about one of the pieces of artwork, for example: 'The green leaves are pinned to the ground to stop them moving. The folds in the leaves make a ridge.'

● Choose one of the pieces of artwork from the website and model how to make notes about it under the headings given on photocopiable page 36 'Plant art'. Give each child a copy of the photocopiable sheet and a small image of the artwork they are going to write about to stick on it. Ask them to complete the sheet by turning the notes they have made into a paragraph for each heading. Focus on using the present tense to give information.

● Look at screen 6 of the website and then use this explanation to create either a lino or styrofoam tile print.

Writing activities

● Over a few art lessons, work with the class to produce a variety of artworks using plants as either the stimulus for a piece or as the main material to create a piece. Ensure they know they are going to create a book about their work so that they are observant.

● Photograph the finished pieces of artwork. Show the whole class how to import the photographs into a word-processing document so that text can be added beneath it.

● Remind the children of the note-making that was modelled earlier and ask them to work individually to make notes on one of their pieces of artwork under the same headings.

● Support each child in turning their notes into a simple paragraph for each heading. Remind them about using the present tense. Tell them to write each paragraph under the image they have added to the word-processing document. Demonstrate how to use the underline and bold tools to make the headings stand out. Encourage them to give each page a title.

● When the children have completed a page for each piece of artwork they can print off their work and add front and back covers, page numbers and a contents page.

● Place the completed books in the book corner or library so that other children can read and discuss them.

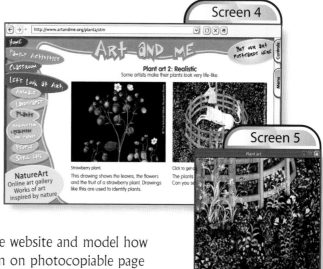

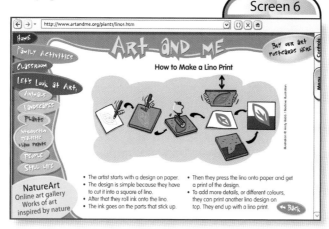

Assessment

● Challenge the children to explain how they reached conclusions about what the website was about. Ask them to highlight the signposts they used, such as the headings and images.

● Look at the children's finished work to assess whether they are able to use the present and passive tenses consistently. Children who are finding this difficult may just recount what they did to create their artwork instead.

Reference to
100 Literacy Framework Lessons

● Non-fiction Unit 4 Non-chronological reports pages 141–156

Photocopiable

● See page 36 or CD-ROM.

A day in the park

Objectives

- Strand 2: Respond to presentations by describing characters, repeating some highlights and commenting constructively.
- Strand 9: Sustain form in narrative, including use of person and time.

Differentiation

Support
- Allow the children to explore alternatives for what could happen at the park through drama. Record their ideas on a large sheet of paper with an adult acting as scribe. If there is a park near to the school, take the children there to do this as it may inspire more coherent ideas.

Extend
- Challenge the children to add two events and resolutions to their stories instead of just one. Support them to plan both events before they begin writing.

Cross-curricular activities

Geography Unit 1
Around our school – the local area
- Draw and label a map of the park from the clues given in the video clip.

How the text works

- This video clip develops visual literacy skills as children learn how to recall and analyse instead of watching passively. Asking children to look for specific things, such as what flavour ice cream the children ate, will make them examine the clip in more detail.

- Watch the clip together and afterwards discuss what it was about. Ask: *Who were the characters? Where did they go? What did they see and do? Did they enjoy their trip to the park?* From the children's direct observations, and also using inference, spend some time describing the characters' appearance and personalities.

- Consider how music affects film. Ask: *What was the mood of the music?* (Happy.) Play the clip again with a sad piece of music imposed. Discuss whether this music is appropriate for the clip and how the music altered the feel of the film.

- Ask the children which part of the clip they liked best and why. Invite them to share their thoughts, first with a partner and then with the class.

Responding to the text

- Evaluate how the clip compares to a book about a visit to the park. Ask: *Could you understand what was happening in the video without words? Which format do you prefer and why?*

- Watch the clip again, then challenge each child to draw a sequence of images to retell the story. When completed, ask them to cut up the sequence and give it to another child to re-order.

- Invite each child to use the re-ordered illustrations to retell the story orally to a partner. Model how to use story

■SCHOLASTIC
www.scholastic.co.uk

language and time connectives to do this. Offer constructive comments: *What was good? How could it be improved next time?*

● In small groups, encourage the children to talk about their own visits to the park. Ask: *Who did you go with? What did you do? Did anything happen while you were there?*

Writing activities

● Explain that a good story follows a four-part sequence: opening, something happens, events to sort it out, ending. Note that the video clip didn't have any really exciting parts and suggest improving one part of the story by following the four-part sequence.

● Consider feeding the ducks. Ask: *What could have happened to make the story more exciting here?* (A swan chases the children, Mum falls into the pond.) Give each pair a copy of photocopiable page 37 'A visit to the park'. Ask them to sequence the pictures correctly then rehearse a simple oral retelling of the events. Encourage the use of story language and time connectives. Point out they should be telling the story in the third-person past tense.

● Allow each pair to present their retellings to the group. Agree a set of success criteria for a good story presentation before the retellings begin and ask the rest of the class to evaluate the presentations against this.

● Model how to write this section of the story. Stress the use of the third-person past tense to tell the story. Include story language, adjectives and suitable time connectives.

● Challenge the children to write an individual story about a trip to the park. Remind them to use the four-part sequence. Support them in planning the story before they begin writing. Invite them to illustrate each part of their story to make it multimodal.

Video © Atmospheres

Assessment

● Can the children recall and sequence a story in the correct order? The initial picture sequencing activity should reveal those children who have difficulty with their visual and auditory sequential memories.

● The children's stories will be limited by their own experiences of visiting the park, so it is important to consider this when assessing their completed work.

Reference to *100 Literacy Framework Lessons*

● Narrative Unit 1 Stories with familiar settings pages 9–30

Photocopiable

● See page 37 or CD-ROM.

Objectives

● Strand 1: Explain ideas and processes using imaginative and adventurous vocabulary and non-verbal gestures to support communication.
● Strand 10: Use appropriate language to make sections hang together.

Differentiation

Support
● Give the children further practice of using connectives by asking them to explain simple everyday processes. Act out some of these processes, taking pictures of each step to order later. When ordering the pictures, use connectives flashcards to link each picture, then use these picture and word clues as prompts to explain the processes verbally.
Extend
● Challenge children who can already use connectives and the present tense to write their own explanation of the life cycle of a tomato plant using just the images as prompts.

Cross-curricular activities

Science Unit 2B
Plants and animals in the local environment
● Ask the children to plant seeds in different conditions to determine the best environment for them to grow into healthy plants. Record the progress of each plant using a flow chart.

The life cycle of an apple tree

How the text works

● This animation incorporates both moving images and sound to illustrate the life cycle of an apple tree. Less confident readers can access this type of text as well as the most confident readers, so they may respond better than expected.

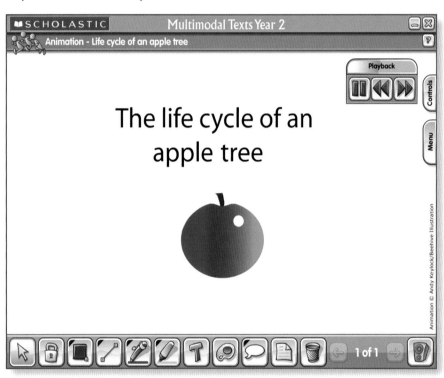

● Talk to the class about where apples come from. Discuss ways in which they could find out about apples in more detail – for example, by using information books, the internet or a DVD, or by asking an adult.

● Watch the animation and allow the children time to discuss what they have found out with a partner. Share a book or web page that explains the life cycle of an apple and compare the two sources of information. Ask: *What are the advantages and disadvantages of each text type? Which did you prefer and why? Could either of the texts be improved in any way to make them easier to follow?*

● Tell the class that the text type they have been studying is an explanation text – that is, a text that explains a process. Point out the use of the present tense and time and causal connectives in both texts.

Responding to the text

● In pairs, ask the children to complete

photocopiable page 38 'The life cycle of a tomato plant'. They must correctly order the life cycle images, then match each of the sentences to the correct image. Also, challenge the pairs to underline all of the present tense verbs (doing or action words) and highlight the time and causal connectives in different colours. They can add arrows to create a flow chart.

- Play the animation without the sound and ask each child to prepare their own verbal explanation to accompany it. Display a word bank of technical vocabulary (shoot, root, grow, soil) and connectives (first, then, next, after that) and challenge the children to try and use them. Ensure they use the present tense.

Writing activities

- Challenge the children to create their own narrated animation using simple animation software, either individually or in pairs.

- Provide some seeded fruit and a blunt knife and encourage each child to find the seeds inside, with adult support. Demonstrate how to plant a seed then tell the class to plant theirs in the same way.

- Invite the children to pick the main six steps of harvesting and planting the seeds and display these clearly. Provide a piece of A3 paper for each child or pair, divided into six, and ask them to illustrate each of the six main steps in order to create a flow chart of the process. Encourage them to add an explanatory sentence to each illustration.

- Support the pairs or individuals in using their flow charts to create a simple animation or series of images that can be narrated. Encourage them to plan their narrations to include all of the text features they have learned about, then record their narrations and attach them to the animations.

- Ask the children to swap their work with another individual or pair and evaluate it by finding three points they think work well and one point that could be improved, giving a suggestion for how this might be done.

Animation © Andy Keylock / Beehive Illustration

Assessment

- When the children are presenting the animation to the class, there will be a good opportunity to assess the use of non-verbal gestures such as pointing. It will also be possible to assess the listening skills of the audience by challenging them to ask the presenter questions after their presentation.
- Many of the time and causal connectives are high frequency words, so this text could be used as an opportunity to assess the children's spelling of these words.

Reference to *100 Literacy Framework Lessons*

- Non-fiction Unit 2 Explanations pages 107–121

Photocopiable

- See page 38 or CD-ROM.

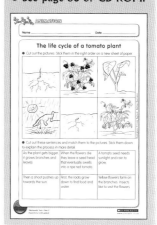

ANIMATION

Objectives

● Strand 1: Tell real and imagined stories using the conventions of familiar story language.
● Strand 8: Engage with books through exploring and enacting interpretations.

Differentiation

Support
● With an adult supporting, the children could role play the beginning of the story to help them decide which choice to make. Extend this by asking them to think collectively of an idea about how the story could end and role play this too.
Extend
● Before reading the ending, challenge the children to write their own ending to the story based on one of the two choices they could make. Give them the beginning of the story with lines beneath it for them to write their ending on. Encourage them to use the past tense and appropriate story language.

Cross-curricular activities

RE Unit 2B
Why did Jesus tell stories?
● Discuss what a parable is. Look at some of the parables from the Bible about things being lost and found, for example the lost sheep, the lost coin and the lost son. Talk about the symbolism used in these stories.

The Ring

How the text works

● This story text offers the children two alternative endings and encourages them to engage fully with the text so that they can make an informed choice about which ending they want.

● Read screen 1 and encourage the class to imagine where the ring came from and who it might belong to. Use small discussion groups to ensure everyone gets the opportunity to put forward their ideas.

● Now read screens 2 to 5. Use the sticky-note tool to display two notes on the whiteboard and ask individuals to describe how each of the characters are feeling about finding the ring. Focus on and develop the children's spelling strategies as they write their ideas.

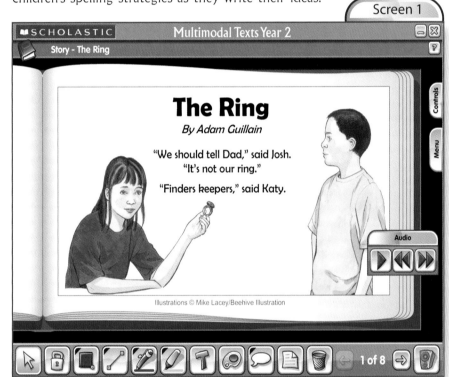

● After reading screen 6, point out that there is now a choice to be made. Explain that the choice made will affect how the story ends. Ask: *Do ordinary paper books offer a choice of ending? What do you think about having a choice? Does it improve the book? Why?*

Responding to the text

● Ask each child to make a brief prediction about what might happen at the end of each scenario. Record some of these ideas to compare to the real endings later.

● Perform a conscience alley with the class to help them decide which choice to make. Split the class into two groups and line them up facing each other then choose a confident child to walk between the two lines. The child walking down the centre must

■SCHOLASTIC
www.scholastic.co.uk

Illustrations © Mike Lacey / Beehive Illustration

Whiteboard tools

● Whiteboard tools used on the screen shots include:
📄 Sticky notes
🔊 Colour used ●

Assessment

● Writing a story from the perspective of another character is quite challenging for some children, so look for those who are struggling and offer them extra support.
● The conscience alley task should give an insight into the children's understanding of cause and effect in stories. Can they imagine what the outcome of their choice might be? Do they appreciate each choice will have a very different ending?

Reference to *100 Literacy Framework Lessons*

● Narrative Unit 1 Stories with familiar settings pages 9–30

Photocopiable

● See page 39 or CD-ROM.

listen to their 'conscience' (the two lines of children) and then make a decision based on what they have heard. One side of their 'conscience' is persuading them to keep the ring and the other side is persuading them to tell Dad about the ring. Read the option chosen.

Writing activities

● Ask each child to imagine they are the person who lost the ring. Explain that they can change the character from the one in the story, and recall their earlier ideas about the ring's owner. Challenge each child to write the story of the lost ring from the perspective of the person who lost it. Give them a copy of photocopiable page 39 'The owner of the ring' to help them plan their story.

● Model the beginning of the story, asking for contributions of ideas from the class. Use appropriate story language and write consistently in the third-person past tense, for example: 'The young woman walked merrily through the park with a pram.'

● Invite the children to work with a partner to tell their story orally before they begin writing. Encourage them to ask questions and make suggestions in order to help their partner improve their story.

● Supply A4 paper folded in half for each child, so that they can write their stories into a book. Give guide lines for the children to write on at the bottom of each page, leaving a space for the illustration at the top. More confident children could even write two alternative endings.

● Place the completed books in the book corner for the class to enjoy. Encourage the readers to tell the authors what they think they did well.

Objectives

● Strand 4: Present part of traditional stories, their own stories or work drawn from different parts of the curriculum for members of their own class.
● Strand 9: Select from different presentational features to suit particular writing purposes on paper and on screen.

Differentiation

Support
● Ask the children to freeze frame the main parts of 'The Monkey and the Lion'. Talk to them about each part of the story in turn and then ask them to work in a small group to create a tableau for each. They could also write dialogue for each character on large speech bubbles made from card and suspend them above the characters' heads.
Extend
● Challenge the children to write a script for their play in a similar style to the playscript on the photocopiable sheet. Look at the use of the narrator to tell the story and the stage prompts that help with acting and expression.

Cross-curricular activities

Design and technology
Unit 2B
Puppets
● Help the children to make simple finger puppets of Rabbit and Fox or Monkey and Lion from felt. They can use them to act out the story from the lesson.

The Rabbit and the Fox

How the text works

● This text offers a comparison between paper-based and electronic story books. The simple text and colourful images make it very accessible to children. You can help the children to read the images as well as the text by asking them to describe what they see happening.

● Introduce the genre of the traditional tale to the class and give some well-known examples such as 'Little Red Riding Hood'. Point out that there are always good and bad characters in these stories and that they sometimes carry a moral.

● Read screen 2 of the story with the whole class. Ask: *What do you think Duck will say?* Sit in a circle and pass around a duck mask so the children can give their answers in role.

● After reading each screen, ascertain how each of the characters would be feeling. Ask: *How did Rabbit feel when he saw Fox was trapped? What about when Fox grabbed him? Do you think Fox was sorry in the end?*

● Discuss the characters' qualities: the friendly, helpful rabbit, the sly fox and the wise duck.

● Look at screen 2 again and ask the children to consider, with a partner, what each of the characters could be saying. Use the speech-bubble tool to share some of these ideas on the whiteboard. Ensure the children understand how and why speech bubbles are used with images.

Responding to the text

● Highlight the main parts of the story by jotting a few key phrases on a timeline. Put the children into groups of three and ask them to act out the story. Give them time to rehearse their ideas then invite them to perform to the rest of the class.

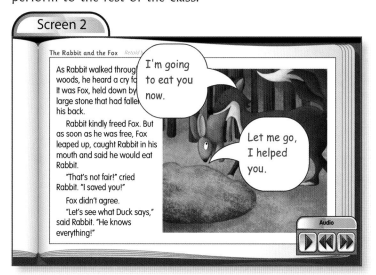

• Give each child a copy of the playscript on photocopiable page 40 'The Monkey and the Lion' and explain how a playscript works. Depending on your class's ability, either ask the children to read the text individually or lead a reading around the class. Compare this second story with 'The Rabbit and the Fox' and note how they are very similar. Also compare the two text types, looking particularly closely at how the dialogue is presented in each text.

Screen 3

Writing activities

• Explain that the children are going to write their own individual traditional story by changing some elements of the two stories they have just read. Show a pre-prepared comic strip of one of the stories that they have already looked at as an example.

• Combine class ideas to create a basic story plan. Decide on three suitable characters – for example squirrel (good), bear (bad) and owl (wise) – and decide on the problem that the bad character is going to have – for example, getting caught in a net. Set the key events out on a simple timeline using key phrases as previously.

• Challenge the children to use the class plan to create individual comic strips of the story. Ensure they have experience of comic strip layouts before they begin. Provide a piece of paper with a box for each key part of the story shown on the timeline plan.

• Support the children in adding speech bubbles to their drawings to help tell the story and also to add a line of narrative to each box to explain the story further.

• Set a list of success criteria with the class before they begin the task and help the children to evaluate the work of their peers against this.

• Challenge the children to work in groups to rehearse and then perform one of their own stories to the rest of the class. Video the performances and show them to other classes. (Remember to get parents' or carers' permission before filming the children.)

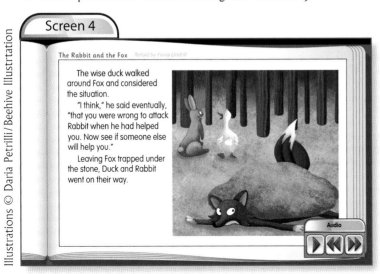

Screen 4

Illustrations © Daria Petrilli/ Beehive Illustration

Whiteboard tools

• Whiteboard tools used on the screen shots include:
  Speech bubble
  Colour used ●

Assessment

• The children's role-play work will provide a good opportunity to assess which children show strengths and weaknesses in presenting story ideas in this manner. Watch carefully for those children who are confident with their dialogue and remain in role throughout.
• The story text can be used to assess children's understanding of the use of speech marks. Those who are assessed to be ready could be introduced to the use of these in their own story writing.

Reference to *100 Literacy Framework Lessons*

• Narrative Unit 2 Traditional stories pages 31–50

Photocopiable

• See page 40 or CD-ROM.

Toads and Diamonds

Objectives

● Strand 9: Draw on knowledge and experience of texts in deciding and planning what and how to write.
● Strand 11: Write simple and compound sentences and begin to use subordination in relation to time and reason.

Differentiation

Support
● Supply the children with puppets and props. Give them time to act out the story in a small group with a supporting adult prompting as necessary.
Extend
● After reading screens 1 to 3 of the story, challenge the children to work in pairs to write the end of the story before they read it. Talk about where they got their ideas from. Was it another story they know? Compare their different endings with the real ending.

Cross-curricular activities

PE Unit 2
Dance activities (2)
● Ask the children to work in groups of four to create a dance that tells the story from the lesson. Encourage them to show the personalities and feelings of the characters through their movements and facial expressions. Choose appropriate music or percussion accompaniment to represent each character.

How the text works and

● Read the story with the children and, at the end of each screen, ask the class to make a prediction about what they think will happen next. Encourage them to explain their answers, giving reasons for their ideas.

● Invite the children to discuss the outcome of the story with a partner. Ask: *Was the ending as you expected? What could have happened instead? How would the end of the story be different if Rosa had got the water for the lady? How do you think each of the sisters is feeling at the end of the story?*

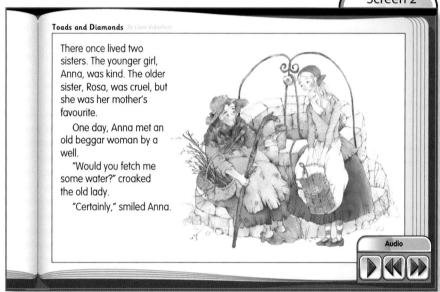

● On each screen, look at the use of story language (*There once lived, happily ever after*) and connectives (*suddenly, and so it was*). Highlight the speech words with the highlighter tool (*said, croaked, smiled, spat*). Ask: *What other speech words could have been used?* Make a word bank of these words to use later on.

Responding to the text

● Sit the children in a circle and explain that they are going to retell the story one sentence at a time. You could pass a toy toad around the circle to signify whose turn it is to speak. Remind them to use story language, dialogue and connectives.

● Consider the characters in more detail. Give the children individual whiteboards and ask them to write describing sentences about each character. Encourage them to use the text and the images in the story to help them. Share their ideas using the sticky-note tool on the whiteboard.

● Children can then use individual whiteboards to create super sentences from basic traditional tale sentences. For example,

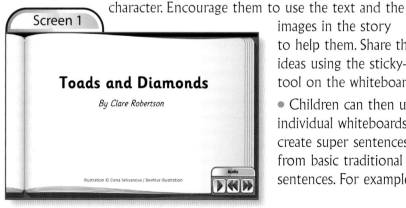

'Tim went for a walk' could become 'One cold autumn morning, Tim, dressed in his warmest clothes, went for a long walk in the forest to find some big conkers so that he could take part in the school conker match.'

Writing activities

- Give each child a copy of photocopiable page 41 'A traditional tale' to support the planning of a new version of the *Toads and Diamonds* story.

- Put the children into groups of four and ask them to generate as many ideas as they can, following the format of the planning sheet. After a while, move two children from each group to another group and ask them to share the ideas they have already discussed. Encourage the new group members to ask questions and add details to improve the ideas.

- Ask each child to complete a planning sheet individually, reminding them that their earlier discussions could give them ideas to use.

- Model how to use a pre-completed planning sheet to support creating a piece of narrative. Emphasise the use of formal story language and time connectives. Remind the whole class how to show dialogue in stories (speech marks, use of alternatives to 'said', showing who is speaking).

- Challenge each child to use their planning sheet to create their own digital story. Use word-processing software to write the narrative, then show the children how to add images and sound to their narrative to make it multimodal.

- Agree a set of success criteria with the class before they begin writing and ask them to evaluate their own completed work against this. Provide a tick list of the criteria for them to complete to support this evaluation. Ask some children to demonstrate where they think they have met the criteria in their work.

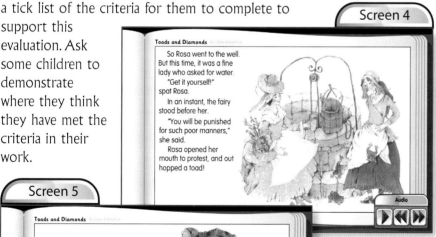

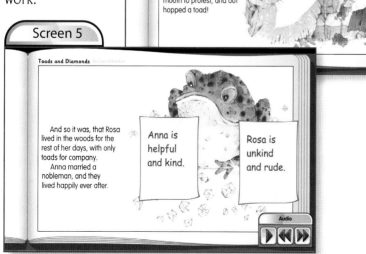

Whiteboard tools

- Whiteboard tools used on the screen shots include:
- 📄 Sticky notes
- 🔵 Colour used ●

Assessment

- This story-writing task provides an excellent opportunity to assess which children are capable of writing more extended narratives. It should provide clear evidence of their ability to use formal story language, dialogue and connectives.
- Underline a few key words that the children have spelt incorrectly in their work and challenge them to correct them. Look closely at the spelling techniques they use to tackle this job.

Reference to *100 Literacy Framework Lessons*

- Narrative Unit 2 Traditional stories pages 31–50

Photocopiable

- See page 41 or CD-ROM.

Objectives

● Strand 3: Ensure that everyone contributes, allocate tasks, and consider alternatives and reach agreements.
● Strand 7: Give some reasons why things happen or characters change.

Differentiation

Support
● When reading the playscript in groups, less confident children could be responsible for providing the sound effects for each group. You could add picture clues to the script to support children who struggle to read.
Extend
● Ask the children to turn their video clip into written narrative as an extra challenge. Remind them to use story language, time connectives and adjectives to describe.

Cross-curricular activities

**Citizenship Unit 2
Choices**
● Sit in a circle and ask the children to say what they like and don't like about playtimes. Make a list of problems that the children have at playtimes and then work together to make a list of ideas for how to solve each of the problems. Remind them that they always have a choice about what they do in the playground.

Skipping and kicking!

How the text works

● Show the children the playscript and explain that it tells the actors in a play what to say and do. Look at how dialogue and stage directions are presented.

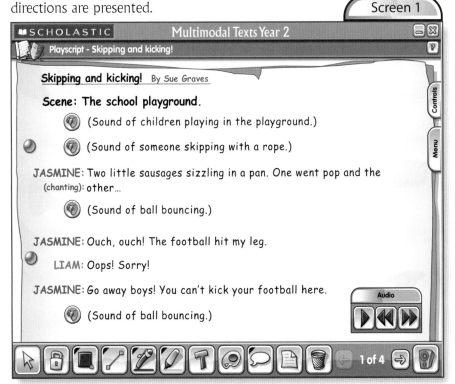

● Listen to the playscript being performed and follow the text on-screen. Ask the class for their reactions. Ask: *Would a playscript in a book have sound effects? Is it easier to read or listen to a playscript? Why?*

● Compare the playscript to a story. Point out that a playscript focuses mostly on dialogue, whereas a story uses description and dialogue.

Responding to the text

● Give each group of four children a copy of the playscript and ask them to practise reading it aloud. Consider the use of expression to make it more interesting to listen to. Evaluate the reading of each group.

● Teach the class that a good story is made up of a four-part sequence: opening, something happens, events to sort it out, ending. Briefly identify these four parts in the playscript. Give each child a copy of photocopiable page 42 'Reading comprehension' and ask them to answer the comprehension questions about the playscript on their own.

● Carry out some hot-seating. Ask a volunteer to imagine they are one of the characters in the play and place them in front of the class with a hat on. Invite the rest of the class to ask the character questions about what happened, what they did, how they felt, how the problem was sorted out and what they would do next time. To begin with, this may need modelling by two adults.

- In a circle, talk with the whole class about their own playground experiences. Pass a teddy around the circle and ask each child to describe a time when they had a problem in the playground and how it was sorted out.

Writing activities

- Ask the children to work with a partner to list problems and solutions that could happen in a school playground setting. Model how to make a record of their ideas in note form under two headings: 'What happens?' and 'How is it sorted out?'

- Combine the pairs to make groups of four and explain that they are going to use some of their ideas to create a video of a story that is set in the school playground. Ensure the groups are of mixed ability.

- Ask the children in each group to pool their ideas and create a storyboard plan using illustrations and captions, following the four-part sequence: opening, something happens, events to sort it out, ending.

- Suggest that the children in each group each take on a role before they begin, ensuring they understand what each role entails – the illustrator creates the storyboard; the director directs the actors and provides dialogue; the camera operator operates the video camera; and the sound effects creator creates the sound effects.

- Provide a video camera and ask each group to create a video of their story from the storyboard they have created. (Remember to get parents' or carers' permission before filming children.) The camera operator should record the performance with the rest of the group as the actors.

- Watch the stories as a class and evaluate their effectiveness. Ask: *Do they follow the four-part sequence? Did it make you want to carry on watching? What was your favourite part? What do you think they did well? What would you have done differently?*

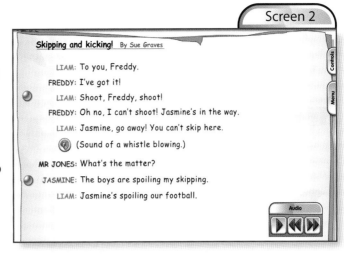

Screen 2

Skipping and kicking! By Sue Graves

LIAM: To you, Freddy.
FREDDY: I've got it!
LIAM: Shoot, Freddy, shoot!
FREDDY: Oh no, I can't shoot! Jasmine's in the way.
LIAM: Jasmine, go away! You can't skip here.
(Sound of a whistle blowing.)
MR JONES: What's the matter?
JASMINE: The boys are spoiling my skipping.
LIAM: Jasmine's spoiling our football.

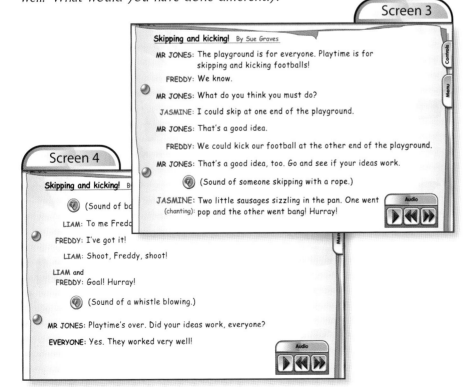

Screen 3

Skipping and kicking! By Sue Graves

MR JONES: The playground is for everyone. Playtime is for skipping and kicking footballs!
FREDDY: We know.
MR JONES: What do you think you must do?
JASMINE: I could skip at one end of the playground.
MR JONES: That's a good idea.
FREDDY: We could kick our football at the other end of the playground.
MR JONES: That's a good idea, too. Go and see if your ideas work.
(Sound of someone skipping with a rope.)
JASMINE: Two little sausages sizzling in the pan. One went (chanting): pop and the other went bang! Hurray!

Screen 4

Skipping and kicking! B

(Sound of b
LIAM: To me Fredd
FREDDY: I've got it!
LIAM: Shoot, Freddy, shoot!
LIAM and
FREDDY: Goal! Hurray!
(Sound of a whistle blowing.)
MR JONES: Playtime's over. Did your ideas work, everyone?
EVERYONE: Yes. They worked very well!

Assessment

- The making of the film should highlight those children who are confident at speaking and performing in front of others. It should also show those who are good at leading and organising, those who can give and receive instructions and those who find it challenging to work alongside other children effectively.
- Look for good use of emphasis and expression when the children are reading the playscript aloud.

References to *100 Literacy Framework Lessons*

- Narrative Unit 1 Stories with familiar settings pages 9–30

Photocopiable

- See page 42 or CD-ROM.

PLAYSCRIPT

Name   Date

Reading comprehension

1 What is Jasmine doing at the beginning of the story?

2 Why did Liam say 'sorry' to Jasmine?
Because he pushed her   Because Jasmine looked sad
Because the ball hit her leg   Because the teacher told him to

3 How do you think Freddie felt when Jasmine was in the way of his game?

4 Who is Mr Jones?

5 What problem did the children have?

6 How did the children sort out their problem?

7 Why did the children feel happy at the end of playtime?

Football in the park

How the text works and responding to the text

● This rhyming poem about football should hold the interest of reluctant boy readers. The twist at the end adds extra interest. The poem's rhyme and rhythm patterns can be heard clearly as it is read aloud.

● Listen to screen 1 of the poem. Discuss why lines 3 and 4 were read in a panting voice. (The sound matches the content of the words.) Ask: *Did you notice any other places where this happened?* (*Howl* on line 6.)

● Now listen to screens 1 and 2. Ask each child to draw a new illustration for one of the pages that includes the players. Encourage the use of discussion with a partner to establish what clues there are in the text that they can use to help them.

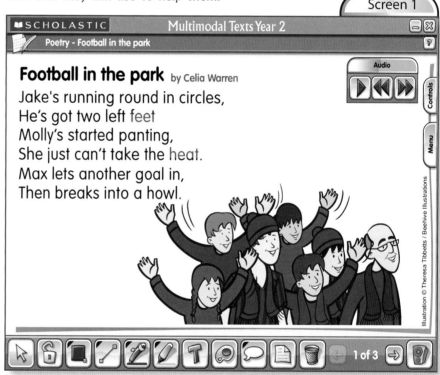

● Read screen 3 of the poem and note that it follows a different pattern from the first two pages. Ask: *Were you surprised that the players were dogs?* Look back at the text for clues that implied this (*howl, panting, bite, running round in circles*) and list them on the screen using the sticky-note tool.

● Split the class in half. Ask one half of the class to practise reciting the poem. Encourage them to focus on their expression and intonation. Remind them of the way the poem was read on-screen. Ask the other half of the class to invent actions to accompany the poem. Combine the two groups' work then swap roles so all the children attempt both tasks.

● Look at the poem again and ask the class to find rhyming words. Highlight the words with the highlighter tool. Look at the pattern the rhyming words follow on each page and note the change in pattern on the final page. Explain that a pair of rhyming lines is called a rhyming couplet.

● Focus on one pair of rhyming words, for example *sight* and *bite*. Look at the graphemes for each word ending – 'ight' and 'ite' – and explain

that these are both ways of writing the same sound. Think of other words that rhyme with *sight* and list them under the appropriate word ending. Repeat this for the other rhyming word families.

- Give each child a copy of photocopiable page 43 'The animal Olympics' and ask them to match two lines together to create a rhyming couplet. Invite them to read and then illustrate each rhyming couplet.

Screen 2

Football in the park by Celia Warren
Jo ignores the whistle
Although she's played a foul.
Billy's keeping the ball to himself,
His dribbling's quite a sight,
But Matty dare not tackle him;
He has been known to bite!

Audio
Controls
Menu

- howl
- panting
- bite
- running round in circles

Illustration © Theresa Tibbetts / Beehive Illustrations

Writing activities

- Create a class rhyming poem about the animal Olympics. First, build an animal word bank. Think of more unusual animals, such as 'platypus' and 'gazelle'. Next, develop a sporting event word bank. Include event names and relevant action words, such as 'hurtled' and 'leaped'. Ask for contributions and also offer some of your own words to help develop new vocabulary.

- Using the word banks, create a rhyming couplet. Construct the first line of the couplet then ask the class to generate rhyming words for the last word of the line. Look at the spelling patterns of some of these words. Model the creation of a suitable second line that ends with one of the words the children suggested – for example, 'The tortoise crawled slowly along in his race, Even the tarantula couldn't quicken his pace.'

- Encourage the children to work in pairs to generate rhyming couplets. Check their work regularly as this task is quite challenging. If it is proving too difficult, provide them with suitable first lines.

- Bring a selection of the class' ideas together in a word-processed document to create a class poem. Leave spaces for each individual to add their own illustrations.

- Supply a copy of the poem to each child and ask them to practise reading it aloud. Focus again on expression and intonation. Record the children reading their poem as a class and attach the recording to the electronic version of the poem.

Assessment

- A child who can generate a rhyming word cannot necessarily put that rhyming word at the end of a suitable line as this requires knowledge of a variety of sentence structures.
- Can the children suggest alternative graphemes for a given phoneme? The nature of these rhyming activities offers a good opportunity to assess the children's ability to do this by asking them to create families of rhyming words.

Reference to
100 Literacy Framework Lessons

- Poetry Unit 1 Patterns on the page pages 157–168

Photocopiable

- See page 43 or CD-ROM.

Screen 3

Audio
Controls
Menu

Football in the park by Celia Warren
Sam is rolling on his back,
He's really muddied his togs,
But it's no surprise
When the teams comprise
Seven scruffy dogs.

Illustrations © Theresa Tibbetts/Beehive Illustration

Illustration © Theresa Tibbetts / Beehive Illustrations

Creating together

Objectives

- Strand 2: Listen to others in class, ask relevant questions and follow instructions.
- Strand 9: Draw on knowledge and experience of texts in deciding and planning what and how to write.

Differentiation

Support

- Ask the children to create a simple model from a construction kit. Help them to record an instruction onto a tape each time they complete a step. Give the rest of the class access to the tape recording and construction kit and see if they can follow the instructions given.

Extend

- Children needing a further challenge could use a tape recorder or the sound recorder on the computer to create their own art and craft show podcast.

Cross-curricular activities

Design and technology Unit 2A

Vehicles

- Children can make a model vehicle and then write a set of instructions for how to make it for another child to follow.

RE Unit 2C

Celebrations

- Discuss the festival or celebration for which the card was made.

How the text works and responding to the text

- This text is a podcast of a children's art and craft radio show. It is a 'listen and do' show. Children could either listen to this alone or with an adult to help them.

- Explain that a podcast is a sound file that can be downloaded from the internet and played on a computer or MP3 player. Listen to the whole podcast. Ask: *What do you think the podcast was about? Have you ever heard anything similar? How could we use this podcast?*

- Explain that the podcast is giving instructions about how to make a puppet. Listen again to confirm this. Provide the

Creating together	
	puppet of a character called Little Red Riding Hood.
Calvin	So what do we need Sophie?
Sophie	You will need red and pink felt, yellow or brown wool, small goggly eyes, card, PVA glue, plain paper, a pencil, felt-tipped pens and some scissors.
Calvin	So when we've collected all these things what do we have to do with them?
Sophie	First make a paper template for the puppet. Draw around

materials to follow the instructions and ask each child to follow them. Ask: *Can you remember everything you need to do?* Suggest replaying the podcast and pausing after each instruction.

- Compare the puppets and evaluate whether the instructions were clear and easy to follow. Ask: *Would it be easier to follow written or drawn instructions or a combination or these?*

- Read and display photocopiable page 44 'How to make an Aboriginal-style shaker'. Look at the language and layout features — the statement of purpose, the list of materials needed, the sequential steps, the direct imperative register (bossy words), and the time connectives.

- Encourage the children to work in pairs to highlight the time connectives in one colour and the bossy words in another colour. They can then follow the instructions to make the shaker.

Writing activities

- Create a word bank of time connectives with the class for them to refer to and display these prominently in the classroom.

Creating together	
Sophie	Next, join the front and back pieces together. Only put glue around the seams and remember not to stick the bottom together because that's where your finger goes in.
	After the glue has dried, cut out a small circle from the pink felt and stick it on the front as a face. Add two goggly eyes and draw on a red mouth with a thin felt-tipped pen.
	Then cut some short strands of wool and glue them onto the puppet to make the hair.

■SCHOLASTIC
www.scholastic.co.uk

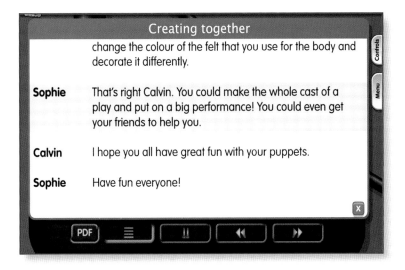

Creating together

	change the colour of the felt that you use for the body and decorate it differently.
Sophie	That's right Calvin. You could make the whole cast of a play and put on a big performance! You could even get your friends to help you.
Calvin	I hope you all have great fun with your puppets.
Sophie	Have fun everyone!

- If possible, ask another adult to demonstrate how to make a card for an appropriate celebration such as Christmas, Hanukkah, Eid or Divali. Include steps that involve sticking pieces on or cutting pieces out, instead of completing a simple drawing. Ask the class to give an instruction for each step after its completion and model how to write this. Take a photograph of the completed card to include in the written instructions.

- Ask the children to work individually to create a card of their own design for the same celebration.

- Encourage individuals to use their own experience to word process a set of instructions for how to make a card, considering language and layout features. Ensure they know how to use the return key to start a new line and how to use the bold and underline buttons for headings. Demonstrate how to use the spell checker if appropriate.

- To make the text multimodal, add a sound recording of each child reading their instructions and a photograph of their finished card to the word-processed page.

Assessment

- Ask the children to work in pairs, one giving and the other receiving instructions to make something. Observe their work and assess. Can the children follow simple oral instructions? Can the children give a simple instruction using appropriate language?

Reference to *100 Literacy Framework Lessons*

- Non-fiction Unit 1 Instructions pages 89–106

Photocopiable

- See page 44 or CD-ROM.

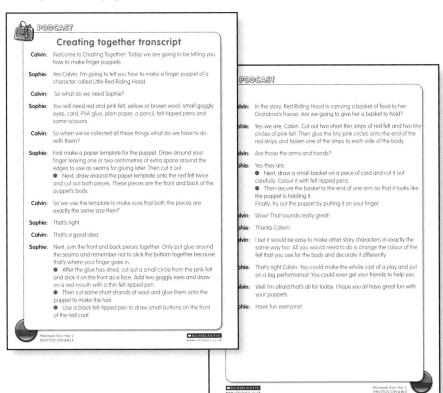

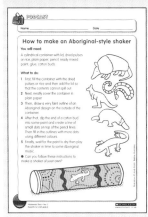

Seaside holiday

Objectives

- Strand 2: Listen to talk by an adult, remember some specific points and identify what they have learned.
- Strand 9: Maintain consistency in non-narrative, including purpose and tense.

Differentiation

Support

- Allow children to role play scenes from a seaside holiday 50 years ago. Support this by suggesting ideas of things the people may have seen and done. Children could work in pairs to produce a recording of two people talking about their seaside holidays as a child.

Extend

- Ask the children to make a short presentation of their work to the class. Encourage them to consider how they can make their presentation more interesting – for example, by adding pictures – and how they might use gestures to emphasise what they are saying.

Cross-curricular activities

History Unit 3
What were seaside holidays like in the past?

- As homework, ask the children to record interviews with adults at home about their experiences of the seaside.

Geography Unit 4
Going to the seaside

- Discuss the physical and man-made features of a seaside town and whether they have changed over time.

How the text works and responding to the text

- Before listening to the text, supply each child with a piece of A4 paper folded into thirds and ask them to write what they already know about seaside holidays in the past in the first of the three columns. In the second column, ask them to write some questions about what they would like to find out about seaside holidays in the past. Leave the third column blank; this should be used at the end of the topic for the children to answer their own questions and record what else they have learned.

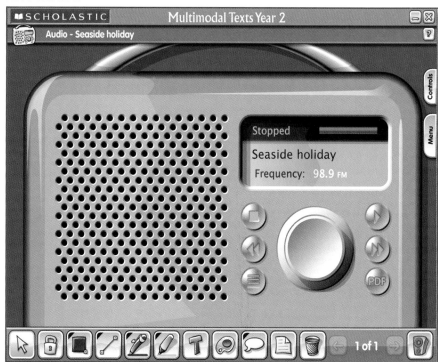

- Play the audio file for the class. Encourage the children to discuss what they have found out with a partner. Play the file again and ask each child to make some quick notes on a piece of paper about seaside holidays in the past. When they have tried to make their notes from the audio, provide them with a copy of the transcript and see if they can find more information from it. Discuss the advantages and disadvantages of each text type.

- Share an information book about seaside holidays in the past with the class as another comparison and again discuss the advantages and disadvantages of each. Look

SCHOLASTIC
www.scholastic.co.uk

at the language and tense used, the page layout of the book, the contents and glossary and how text and images are combined to give information.

● Encourage each child to add to their previously made notes using information gained from the book. Stress to the children that notes should be concise and use only key words and phrases rather than full sentences.

● Support pairs of children in using their notes to create an audio recording of a role play in which a young child interviews one of their grandparents about their experiences of seaside holidays in the past.

Seaside holiday

Child Where did you used to go on your holidays when you were little Dad?

Dad I used to go to Mablethorpe every August.

Child Who did you go with?

Dad Your Gran and Granddad, A Uncle Kevin and my Grandd Grandma Betty. They were Q your great grandparents.

Gran Your Great Granddad Tom u boat out of sand for your da Kevin. It was big enough for inside.

Seaside holiday

Child So you went to the beach every day then?

Dad Mostly we did but we sometimes ate our picnic near the boating lake or spent the afternoon at the children's paddling pools.

Gran We sometimes used to go for a walk in the sand dunes after our picnic lunch as well.

Child Did you do anything else?

Dad After tea in the holiday flat where we were staying, we used to go to the amusements. There were lots of 1p and 2p machines to play on but there weren't really any computer arcade games then. My favourite game was Roll a penny. [X]

Writing activities

● Set the children the task of creating their own information book about seaside holidays in the past. Provide each child with two pieces of A3 paper folded in half and stapled together to make a book. This can include a front cover, a contents page, four information pages, a glossary and a back cover. Rule with lines if necessary.

● Ask each child to create a front cover for their book including author and title. They should write the headings 'Contents' and 'Glossary' on the relevant pages and add page numbers.

● Give each child photocopiable page 45 'Seaside holidays in the past'. Ask them to match up the headings and images and stick each pair on a new page of their information book. Ensure they add the relevant headings to the contents page along with the correct page numbers. Then challenge them to use their notes to write a paragraph of information which is relevant to the page heading and image.

● Ask each child to pick out one word from each page that they would like to include in the glossary and to highlight it. Remind them that the word should be a new or unusual word. Support them to order the words alphabetically and add them to the glossary page with a definition.

Assessment

● Use the note-taking task as an opportunity to find out whether the children can make simple notes from a variety of text sources.
● With the children, create a list of success criteria that you will be looking for when you mark their work and then give them feedback against these agreed criteria at the end of the task.

Reference to *100 Literacy Framework Lessons*

● Non-fiction Unit 3 Information texts pages 123–140

Photocopiable

● See page 45 or CD-ROM.

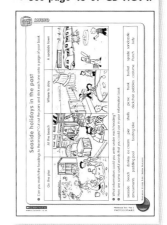

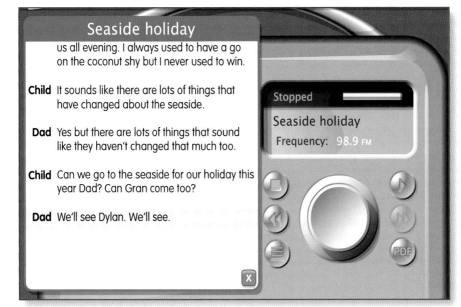

Seaside holiday

us all evening. I always used to have a go on the coconut shy but I never used to win.

Child It sounds like there are lots of things that have changed about the seaside.

Dad Yes but there are lots of things that sound like they haven't changed that much too.

Child Can we go to the seaside for our holiday this year Dad? Can Gran come too?

Dad We'll see Dylan. We'll see.

Stopped

Seaside holiday
Frequency: 98.9 FM

Electricity

How the text works and responding to the text

- This sequence of images provides a starting point for a discussion about electricity. Each image has a sound effect, so discuss with the children how these add to the text as they read it.

Objectives

- **Strand 3:** Work effectively in groups by ensuring that each group member takes a turn challenging, supporting and moving on.
- **Strand 7:** Explain organisational features of texts, including alphabetical order, layout, diagrams, captions, hyperlinks and bullet points.

Differentiation

Support
- Ask the children to choose five suitable key words and to order these alphabetically. Record the children's oral definitions on the computer and incorporate the recordings on a page showing the key word and an image.

Extend
- Challenge the children to create a page of information about electricity that includes their five chosen key words and then to create a glossary page to explain each of the key words. Show them how to create a hyperlink to the glossary pages from the main text page.

Cross-curricular activities

Science Unit 2F
Using electricity
- Children can draw a labelled diagram of a circuit and write a simple explanation of how a torch works using a diagram to help.

History Unit 2
What were homes like a long time ago?
- Use screen 4 to discuss what life was like in homes before electricity.

- Show screen 1 and ask: *What dangers can you see in this room?* (A hanging cord on the iron, a broken socket and light switch, an electrical appliance too near to the sink, an electric carving knife in reach of a child, a knife sticking into a toaster that is plugged in, a lamp without a bulb in.) Put the children into groups and give each group a copy of the image. Ask them to work together to find all of the dangers in the image and to decide on a way to record what they find. Encourage them to take it in turns to suggest and record ideas. Demonstrate how they can challenge ideas they do not agree with in an appropriate and positive way. For example, 'I'm not sure about that one because...', 'Please can you explain why you think that would be dangerous?' Use the whiteboard tools to share each group's ideas.

- Show screen 2 and ask: *What can you see?* Explain that all the appliances are powered by electricity from the mains or a battery. Define these terms. Challenge each child to think of two more electrical appliances and to write these on individual whiteboards. Remind the class of strategies for spelling unfamiliar words. Correct words that are incorrectly spelt together.

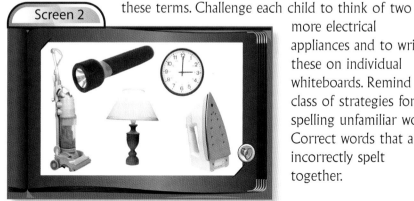

SCHOLASTIC
www.scholastic.co.uk

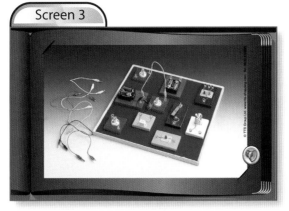

Screen 3

• Show screen 3 and explain that it is a circuit board. As a whole class, label some of the components using the sticky-note tool. Demonstrate how to use a science dictionary to find the correct spellings of these words. Point out that the dictionary is ordered alphabetically to help with finding words. Ask each child to order the word labels alphabetically. Then, ask them to think of other science words related to the topic of electricity and to add these to their list. Provide each child with photocopiable page 46 'Science dictionary' and encourage them to write definitions for each of the words shown, then cut out each word and definition and order them alphabetically.

• Show screen 4 and ask the class to be history detectives. Ask them to work in pairs or small groups to identify the differences between the room in the image and a room today. Ask: *Which of these differences are because we have electricity now?*

Writing activities

• Use the notes made in the screen 1 task to create a group poster or information leaflet detailing how to stay safe around electricity. This can be done on paper or using simple desktop publishing software. Encourage the use of text and suitable images. For example, if a child writes about the dangers of flying a kite near an overhead cable they could add an illustration of someone doing this and the electricity running down the kite wire to their hands.

• Create an electronic dictionary of electricity topic vocabulary. Ask the children to work in pairs to choose and alphabetically order five key words they would like to include in their electricity dictionary. Using suitable software, create a simple template that incorporates a heading box, a text box and an image box for each of the five words chosen. Remind the children to add the words to the heading boxes alphabetically.

Screen 4

Whiteboard tools

• Whiteboard tools used on the screen shots include:
  Pen tool
  Colour used ●

Assessment

• Use the dictionary work as an opportunity to assess whether the children can order alphabetically and use alphabetically ordered texts efficiently.

• During discussion and group work time, look for children who are finding it difficult to participate and offer them extra support. Try to identify the reason for their lack of participation – low self-confidence, speech and language difficulties, poor understanding of the task, behaviour issues, and so on.

Reference to
100 Literacy Framework Lessons

• Non-fiction Unit 3
Information texts
pages 123–140

Photocopiable

• See page 46 or CD-ROM.

An island home

How the text works and responding to the text

- These images illustrate a small Scottish island and give an insight into the lives of the community living there. Screen 1 is a map of the whole island, which shows a variety of geographical features, and the next three screens focus in on specific parts of the island – the bay and village, the coastline and a farmhouse. The sound effects attached to each image add further detail by allowing the viewer to hear the island as well as see it.

- Ask the children: *What would you expect to see on a map of a small Scottish island? How would this be shown on a map?* Look very closely at the map on screen 1. Explain what the key is and how to use it, then ask the class to find all of the features that are shown in the key. Challenge more confident children to find definitions for the features in a dictionary.

- Look at screens 2, 3 and 4. Listen to their sound effects and allow small groups of children to discuss what they can see and hear. Challenge them to find and record two interesting observations from each image. Listen to feedback of discussions from each group and then label the features on each screen, concentrating on spelling techniques.

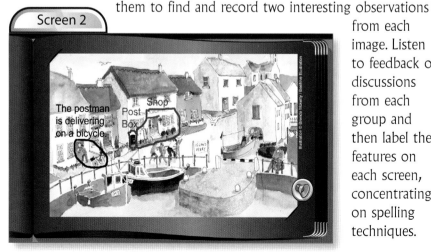

SCHOLASTIC
www.scholastic.co.uk

Screen 3

- Look at a book about life on a Scottish island and compare the two text types. Ask: *How do we find information in each of the texts? How are the two text types different? Which do you prefer and why?*

- Return to screen 1. Choose a feature, such as the village, farm, coastline or mountains, and demonstrate how to write a few simple information sentences about that feature. Divide the children into groups and give each group a copy of photocopiable sheet 47 'A Scottish island home'. Challenge each group to write a few information sentences about each of the features shown on the sheet. Evaluate the sentences as a class and refine them appropriately.

Writing activities

- Invite the children to make a promotional information leaflet encouraging tourists to visit a fictional Scottish island. The leaflet should incorporate text and images.

- Show leaflets from a range of tourist attractions and places of interest. Look at and evaluate the layout of each and how the text is written.

- Working in groups of three, the children can use a large sheet of paper to produce a mind map of what they could include in their leaflet. They should write the name of the Scottish island in the centre of the paper, then each group member can think of one heading they would like to include in their leaflet and write this on a central spur. Encourage them to keep these broad – for example, 'things to see', 'things to do', 'places to stay', 'the coastline', 'the village', and so on. Next, invite the children to write two relevant key words or phrases for each of the headings – for example, for 'things to see' they could write 'castle' and 'lighthouse'. Finally, expanding on these key words, ask group members to write a short phrase that could be expanded upon and included in the leaflet – for example, for 'castle' they could write 'built in 1792'.

- Guide the children into making their own individual leaflets using the mind maps created by their groups. Provide a writing guide with a suitable layout for a leaflet and help them to consider how they could use images to add more detail and clarity to their information.

Screen 4

Assessment

- Check whether particular children can use a dictionary by asking them to find the definitions of the geographical words independently.
- Take note of children's preferences for text types during discussion as this may give some clues to their learning style or suspected learning difficulties.
- Look at the children's completed leaflets and assess whether they have been able to use the notes made by their group effectively. Have they included everyone's ideas or just their own?

Reference to *100 Literacy Framework Lessons*

- Non-fiction Unit 3 Information texts pages 123–140

Photocopiable

- See page 47 or CD-ROM.

Name _____

Date _____

Cars on a ramp

- Use illustrations and captions to show what you did in your experiment.

Name _____

Date _____

Clean-up day

What should you wear on a clean-up day?

● _____

● _____

● _____

● _____

● _____

● _____

● _____

● _____

● _____

● _____

Keeping children safe on clean-up day

● _____

● _____

● _____

● _____

● _____

● _____

● _____

● _____

● _____

● _____

How to organise a clean-up day

● _____

● _____

● _____

● _____

● _____

● _____

● _____

● _____

● _____

● _____

Name _____ Date _____

Plant art

About the art work _____

_____

_____

Materials _____

_____

_____

How it was made _____

_____

_____

Name _____ Date _____

A visit to the park

● Cut out the pictures and put them in the correct order.

Illustrations © Andy Robb/ Beehive Illustration

● Here are some ideas for how to start your story.

> One sunny day…   As the clock chimed 10 o'clock…
> It was a lovely day so…   Last Spring…   Early one afternoon…

● Here are some useful time connectives that you could use in your retelling.

> Meanwhile   Next   Then   After a while   Suddenly
> Finally   Eventually   While   Before

Name _____   **Date** _____

The life cycle of a tomato plant

● Cut out the pictures. Stick them in the right order on a new sheet of paper.

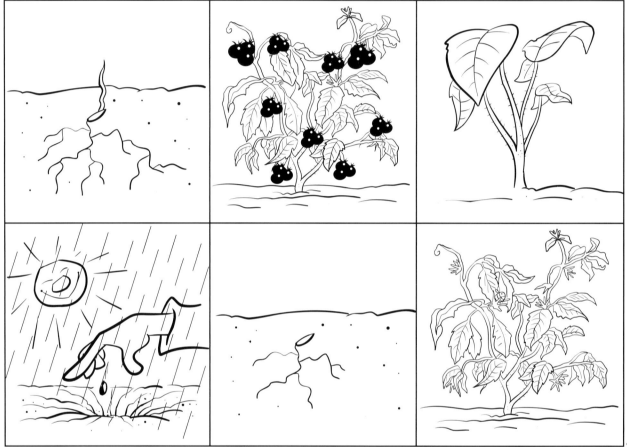

Illustrations © Andy Keylock / Beehive Illustration

● Cut out these sentences and match them to the pictures. Stick them down to explain the process in more detail.

As the plant gets bigger, it grows branches and leaves.	When the flowers die they leave a seed head that eventually swells into a ripe red tomato.	A tomato seed needs sunlight and rain to grow.
Then a shoot pushes up towards the sun.	First, the roots grow down to find food and water.	Yellow flowers form on the branches. Insects like to visit the flowers.

Name _____ **Date** _____

The owner of the ring

Describe the person who owns the ring. _____

_____

_____

Why was this person in the park? _____

_____

_____

How did the owner lose the ring? _____

_____

_____

Why is the ring special to the owner? _____

_____

_____

How did the owner feel when they realised they had lost the ring? _____

_____

_____

What did the owner do? _____

_____

_____

How did they get the ring back? _____

_____

_____

STORY

The Monkey and the Lion

Scene 1

NARRATOR: As Lion was walking through the jungle he fell into a hole. Monkey heard Lion shouting for help.

LION: HELP ME! I'm stuck down this big hole.

MONKEY: (nervously) I will help you as long as you promise not to hurt me.

LION: I won't hurt you Monkey. I will be your friend.

NARRATOR: Monkey helped Lion out of the hole but as soon as he had done this Lion caught Monkey's tail in his teeth.

LION: Now I'm going to eat you. I'm so hungry after being in that hole.

MONKEY: (worriedly) That's not fair! You promised you wouldn't hurt me!

LION: Maybe I've changed my mind.

MONKEY: Let's go and see Elephant and ask him what he thinks.

Scene 2

NARRATOR: They found Elephant and explained what had happened.

MONKEY: Can you help us Elephant?

ELEPHANT: Show me the hole that Lion was trapped in.

NARRATOR: Lion and Monkey led Elephant to the hole.

ELEPHANT: Lion, show me exactly where you were when Monkey found you.

NARRATOR: Lion jumped back into the hole and Elephant looked down at him.

ELEPHANT: (thoughtfully) I think that you were wrong to try and eat Monkey after he helped you. I wonder if there's anyone else in this jungle kind enough to help you like Monkey did?

NARRATOR: Monkey and Elephant went on their way leaving Lion trapped in the hole again.

Name _____   Date _____

A traditional tale

● Draw the characters in your story. Give each character a name.

Good character	Bad character	Magical character

Where does the story take place? _____

What does the good character do to be rewarded? _____

What was the reward? _____

What does the bad character do to be punished? _____

What was the punishment? _____

How does the story end? _____

Name _____   Date _____

Reading comprehension

1 What is Jasmine doing at the beginning of the story?

_____

2 Why did Liam say 'sorry' to Jasmine?

Because he pushed her. ☐   Because Jasmine looked sad. ☐

Because the ball hit her leg. ☐   Because the teacher told him to. ☐

3 How do you think Freddie felt when Jasmine was in the way of his game?

_____

4 Who is Mr Jones? _____

_____

5 What problem did the children have? _____

_____

6 How did the children sort out their problem? _____

_____

7 Why did the children feel happy at the end of playtime? _____

_____

Name _____ **Date** _____

The animal Olympics

● Can you match two lines together to make a rhyming couplet?

Zoe Zebra couldn't win her race,
She finished first and she felt great!
Tess Tortoise felt her tummy curdle,
But he sweats a lot and it makes him pong!
When Tiger Tim leaped very high.
When she saw the height of the first hurdle.
The weightlifting Walrus is very strong,
Sal Snake slithered down the home straight,
As Charlie Cheetah had a faster pace.
The crowd let out an excited cry,

Illustrations © Theresa Tibbetts/ Beehive Illustration

How to make an Aboriginal-style shaker

You will need:

A cylindrical container with lid, dried pulses or rice, plain paper, pencil, ready-mixed paint, glue, cotton buds.

What to do:

1 First, fill the container with the dried pulses or rice and then add the lid so that the contents cannot spill out.

2 Next, neatly cover the container in plain paper.

3 Then, draw a very faint outline of an Aboriginal design on the outside of the container.

4 After that, dip the end of a cotton bud into some paint and create a line of small dots on top of the pencil lines. Then fill in the outlines with more dots using different colours.

5 Finally, wait for the paint to dry then play the shaker in time to some Aboriginal music.

● Can you follow these instructions to make a shaker of your own?

Illustrations © Andy Robb/ Beehive Illustration

Seaside holidays in the past

● Can you match the headings to the images? Cut out the pairs and stick each one onto a page of your book.

On the pier	At the beach	Where to stay	A seaside town

● What information could you write under each heading?

● Here are some useful words that you could use in your information book:

seaside   beach   donkey   ice cream   pier   shells   picnic   trunk   bucket   spade   sandcastle

amusements   paddling pool   boating lake   deckchair   pebbles   costume   Punch   Judy

Illustrations © Andy Robb/ Beehive Illustration

Name _____   **Date** _____

Science dictionary

● Write a definition for each of these science words then cut out and order the words alphabetically.

waterproof _____	
insect _____	
force _____	
battery _____	
ruler _____	
melt _____	

● When you have finished, swap your work with a friend and use a science dictionary to check that their definitions are correct.

Name _____

Date _____

A Scottish island home

● Can you write some information sentences about each of these features?

The farmhouse	The village green	Sandy Beach

Illustrations © Brenda McKetty / Beehive Illustration

SCHOLASTIC

Also available in this series:

ISBN 978-0439-94577-6

ISBN 978-1407-10013-5

ISBN 978-1407-10014-2

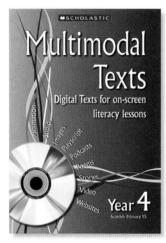

ISBN 978-1407-10015-9

ISBN 978-1407-10016-6

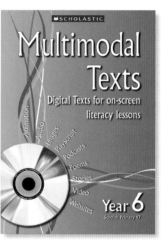

ISBN 978-1407-10017-3

To find out more, call: 0845 603 9091
or visit our website www.scholastic.co.uk